Happy

The Learning Curve

Tim Curry

ISBN 978-1-62806-375-2   (print | paperback)

Library of Congress Control Number 2023907627

Cover image and graphics by Tim Curry

All interior photographs by Tim Curry; bi-plane graphic used with proper permission from istockphoto.com

The Learning Curve

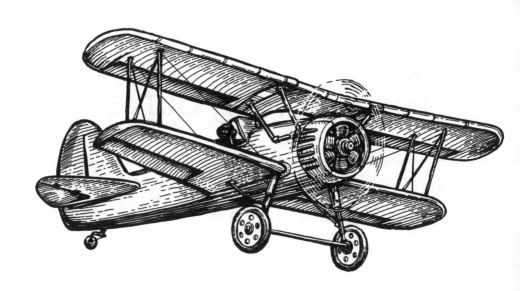

Dedication

Jennifer Curry Tawes, my youngest sister, that was always there. Even though I was her older brother, she seemed to think that her job was to take care of me, always wanting to know if I needed anything, anything at all. She was always ready to help anyone in need. I knew that whatever I did, good or bad, I would have her unconditional forgiveness and love. We all miss her very much!

Contents

Acknowledgements

Kay, my wife, who finds security in the status-quo, is very much against my new adventures. But once I start the next undertaking, she is always been one hundred and ten percent behind me, if not out in front. Without all her support and great enthusiasm, I don't think the business would have reached such a level of success. She has been involved in everything from billing, driving trucks, holding various parts while I bolted them together, picking up materials, and she was almost always my chemical mixer. During the seeding season, she climbs up on the plane, opens a tank lid, holds the shoot, closes the lid, wipes off the windshield every load, often sixty times a day, sometimes does all of this for more than one plane, not to mention taking phone messages and bossing the help.

Kris, our grandson and my sidekick, has been with us throughout this adventure. He was about eight when he accompanied me at the first farm auction buying gas tanks, pumps, hoses, etc. On weekends he helped me build a load center, then helped me haul that load center to Bennett Airport for the start of this adventure. As he got a little older, he would help with loading, engine changes, maintenance, rebuilding planes, and everything else involved. We enjoyed our road trips down south every couple of years to buy planes and plane parts.

My mother has been supportive throughout this whole adventure and is always in the background. A retired schoolteacher, she served as my editor. Much like my school days, she marked up my papers with a red marker. This many years later, whatever writing skills I may have ever had are very rusty, which meant thousands of red marks on this manuscript. Thanks, Mom!

Author's Note

Even though this is the beginning, it was just about the last of my writing. The stories came easy; I had tried to remember all the different events, but for some reason this introduction was more difficult to write. Not knowing how to write an introduction, I picked up many books and tried to find one to use as a model. Most were boring and lengthy, and in thinking back, I normally skip the introduction. After questioning friends and family, most said they really don't read them either. I did want this to be a proper book, so I am including an introduction, but it's going to be quick.

So often aviation memoirs start with a statement like this: "For as long as I can remember even as a young child, all I ever wanted to do is fly." But really, this isn't true for me. However, I took an interest in flight from time to time, building balsa-wood airplanes that were supposed to fly and normally met a disastrous end. Rick, a neighbor and sometimes babysitter, took my father and me flying, which did spark some interest. Still, whatever interest I occasionally had was more about making things fly rather than flying. I didn't have this burning desire to fly like many other writers mention; heck, for a while, as an older teenager, I couldn't find enough ambition to get out of bed each morning, let alone have some grand plan for the future. It has been said that if my head had been on fire and I was holding a glass of water, I never would have found the gumption to lift the water to put out the fire. Yet somehow, I managed to grow out of it and even became a bit of a workaholic. However, once the flying bug bit me at age 28, I was totally consumed by it and have loved every minute of it since.

It is important to remember most of these events took place when phones were attached to the wall with a cord, and maps were made of paper. Although things like computers, cellphones, the internet, GPS, the short-lived pager, or availability to have weather radar may have been invented or in the process thereof, these things were not widely available at that time. Without all the readily available information of today, the learning curve was much more pronounced.

After reading this, most would be afraid to let me fly a kite, let alone get in a plane with me. How could he possibly be successful? Just remember that writing about all the things that went right would be boring. My aviation career has been an absolute joy. To my astonishment, we were able to prosper and make a good living. We now live in the middle of our own hundred-acre farm in a beautiful new home and have our own runway, with all kinds of toys, and more importantly, all the great friends that we made traveling this adventure.

This writing is about many different events and reads like a series of short stories, rather than a novel. Occasionally some of the stories will not be mentioned in the order the event took place, but rather paired with similar events.

Chapter 1
Growing Wings

On my 28th birthday, Mom gave me a gift certificate for an introductory flight at the local airport. One nice sunny Saturday afternoon, it was time to cash it in. Before taking the flight the instructor, Stew, asked if I was serious about taking lessons or if I just wanted to go up and fly around a bit. I said I wished to continue with lessons, so he gave me a book and told me to read the first three chapters, then come back and he would give me a real lesson. As I would learn later, there seemed to be three good ways of starting an aviation career. The first and easiest is to have wealthy parents who can afford to send you to one of those Florida flight schools like Embry-Riddle. The second and best is to go through the military services. Later in life, after meeting all the great guys that I know with unbeatable training and experiences, my biggest regret is I didn't go into the service, but at that time, I wasn't exactly college material. The last way and the route that I would have to take is after the family comes along and you're working like a dog, is to start taking lessons, one lesson at a time, whenever you can scrape up a few bucks or rob the family budget. This route will take a while, and you may find that your better half doesn't always share your enthusiasm. It took me about a year and a half just to get the private pilot license. Another guy, Rob, much younger than me, started about the same time and was able to go straight through, getting his license in about six weeks, then went down south and got all his ratings. Rob ended up being my last instructor, prepping me for the check ride, although I'm not sure how much he taught me. Whenever I would bounce one in, he would just laugh and say that was the worst landing ever, but we had a good time.

AFTER a Friday evening lesson practicing takeoffs and landings, Stew jumped out of the plane and said, "Give me three good ones," with that, I soloed. Much to my surprise it went pretty well, but I did notice that the seat and yoke were covered in sweat when I got out, and I'm not the nervous sweaty type. In fact, as an electrician, my hands are so dry I don't feel much when touching hot wires, and I enjoyed watching my peers holler and jump around after touching that same wire which they thought was off since it didn't seem to bother me. But I sure worked up a sweat on that solo. After that solo flight, Stew signed me off to fly solo as a student pilot, then told me to go ahead take a solo practice flight and just have a good time before we bear down on the next lesson. The next morning as I was getting the plane ready, Stew came out and instructed me to have a good time and stay within twenty-five miles. That's exactly what I did; just like a dog breaking loose from its leash, I buzzed everybody I could think of, being careful not to be seen by other planes. I found a house under construction that my guys were wiring, so I buzzed them. John the electrician ran out into the front yard, seeing him I doubled back and made a run on him, as I pulled up and looked out the back window, he was lying flat on the ground, he told me later the plane looked huge, (it was a small Cessna one-fifty); After that, I flew along the Nanticoke river just a few feet above it, under the Vienna power plant wires, all the way to the Chesapeake Bay. Twice Stew told me to have a good time, and so I did. When I returned, Stew called me into his office, then slammed the door shut; he was very agitated, raising his voice. "Flying a little bit low, weren't you?" Not being able to come up with a good answer, I just responded, "Well yes, I was, but how did you know?" I had no idea that the noise of a plane too close to chicken houses will scare the chickens and they will run to one end and smother each other. Apparently, the airport phone was ringing off the hook from all the chicken farmers. Many years later, when I stopped in the Laurel airport, I notice that the door going to that side office still had the crack in the glass from Stew angrily slamming it shut that day. After that, every time I would preflight a plane ready to go solo, Stew would come running out and tell me, "You stay away from those damn chicken houses."

Stew was pretty strict and never joked around, never seemed to be happy with whatever I did. Sometimes I would just grease in a landing so good you wouldn't know you had landed until you realized the plane had just quit moving. And then Stew would start in "now back on downwind why did you adjust the power before applying carb heat?" and so on. As we were reviewing charts before my first night cross-country, he quizzed me, "Now what do you do if the engine quits?" I gave all the right answers, like follow the emergency checklist, set up the best glide speed, and so on. He added, "now right before you land turn on the landing light." Weighing every word this serious man said, I replied "yeah and what next," he said, "well if you don't like what you see, turn the light back off." Wow! Stew got me, hook, line, and sinker! We flew somewhere up in Pennsylvania, and on the way back it started snowing. I thought it was beautiful. But Stew was nervously shining a flashlight all around on the wings, looking for ice and calling Dover Approach asking temperature and wind. I just flew along, all fat, dumb, and happy. We made it home fine, but I never saw someone squirm in their seat so much worrying about ice.

One winter day, while still a student, I was just itching to fly. I hadn't flown for at least a month, the wind was twenty-five to thirty at a direct crosswind to the runway. As I walked into the office to get the keys and clipboard, a couple of guys that were always hanging out at the airport, Bruce that had a Piper 6, and Mark, who had a Piper twin, both warned me against flying that day. I got out of there before they phoned Stew to tell me not to go. At about the first third of the runway to the north, they had trenched in a wire, and it had made a little hump. I had made a habit to land behind the trees before the hump, so that hump wouldn't throw me back in the air just as the plane touched down. This day I did the same. While rolling out from behind the trees, the wind struck the right side of the small plane with such force as to blow me off to the left. The plane damn near hit a building. I had just missed the hanger by less than a foot! On the "Oh shit" scale it was a #1. (The "Oh shit" scale is how many times you can say "Oh shit" before an imminent impact or some kind of horrific fiery crash, and a "Holy shit" is just off the scale). I haven't decided whether falling off a tall building being able to say, "Oh shit" a lot of times before impacting the earth is better than simply getting unexpectedly shot and never, ever getting one "Oh shit" out. Now if you can stretch out the "Oh" like "Ooooohhh shit," that means there is a pretty good chance of a near miss and coming out alive. Anyways, enough with the profanities and back to the story: it was a #1. After that, all I could think was let me the hell out of this s.o.b. By the time I taxied back to the parking spot, I had built up more nerve and decided to get back on the horse, and I did eight more landings, improving on crosswind landings and takeoffs greatly.

On one of my last solo cross-countries, while going into Norfolk, the controller told me I was "Cleared to land, make it short," I thought what in the hell he meant by make it short, then I looked out the back window to see a Boeing 737 was gaining on me fast. I made that little Cessna touch down right on the numbers at just about full speed, then tried to turn off on the first taxiway. Just then the left wing went way up, and the plane almost flipped over. Trying to save it, it rocked the other way, and the right wing went way up, and then back up on the first wing. Finally I got control. I think that on the "Oh shit" scale it was a #2. Maybe next time, I will request to let the other guy go first.

Getting through the rest of the private license was uneventful. My check ride was a piece of cake; the examiner kept looking at his watch the whole time, and shortly after getting started, he announced, "That's enough. I have a dentist appointment."

The great thing about taking all those lessons and practicing is that I was going through a rough spot in my construction business and the bills were piling up. This was during the days when Jimmy Carter was President, the interest rates were sixteen or seventeen percent, you couldn't sell the Taj-Mahal for five cents. When I was flying, all the earthbound stress disappeared: looking down at the nice, neat squares of towns, forest land, and different colors of the farm fields, everything looked in order. I realized that I could barely see or make out the small part of the earth that consumed my daily life. My world was just a tiny piece of what you see from that vantage. Why get hung up on one little problem that can't even be seen from here when there is so much more, even beyond the horizon. Later around 2005, when I was no longer in the construction business, a building boom occurred, and I could have sold a doghouse for a hundred thousand; oh well, so goes life.

SATURDAY night, just a few days after I received my private pilot license, together three friends and I, rented a Piper Warrior, a marginal four-seater, which means it has four seats but may not carry four people with full tanks. Unfortunately, the fuel was topped off for the renters booked before us that had canceled. I knew it was probably overweight, so I'd just have to be sure to keep the speed up. We headed out for Atlantic City for a night on the town and would land at the small downtown airport called Bader, where Trump keeps his chopper, and a taxicab only cost two dollars to get to the casinos. At that time, Bader had an active control tower, requiring us to call before entering their airspace; however, they were under the Atlantic City International airspace and it was necessary to call them first. Talking on the radio has been my weak point: I've been very much intimidated by it. I took too long to switch over from A.C. Int. to Bader, and that put us right on top of them when calling in, confusing the controller, who thought we were out of the south when we really were out of the west. He had us flicking on and off the landing light to see where we were. He made it easy to detect the hostility in his voice, then told us to turn downwind: "you are number two." When downwind, that plane should continue that heading until abreast of the plane on final before turning base, so this is what I was doing; I kept looking for a plane but couldn't see it. Finally, we spot a nice looking Piper Dakota a lot lower than anticipated going between two casinos and landing. I told the guys that didn't look safe and that I would go over the buildings. Now turning final at just about eight hundred feet, we were almost on top of the airport. After muddling up all the previous radio conversations, I wasn't going to call that intimidating man on the radio and tell him I'd have to go around, so I would just have to make the best of it. I put full flaps and had the really beautiful left slip going, touched down deep, then pulled the flaps off to put the weight on the wheels, and was riding the breaks hard. You could see the line of red lights at the end of the runway coming up fast, beyond that was the bay, stopping in time was going to be tight, so I got the plane to the left side and prepared to loop to the right if needed so as not to go in the water. Luckily, the plane came to a stop, and we still had two or three inches to spare. Because of the hard turn I made, and the freezing temperatures, the left strut was down and stayed down, so as we taxied to our parking spot, the plane stayed tilted to the left. A van came out and picked us up, as well as the ones in the Dakota that we followed in. By now the guys were regaining their speech, Kevin turned to me and asked "what the hell kind of landing was that? I was looking out the side window, and the plane was going sideways towards the runway." As I started to explain that's called a slip, the lady in the front, who was in the other plane, obviously well to do, wearing a mink coat and more gold jewelry than Mister T, asked me how many hours do you have? Not thinking fast enough to lie, I replied, "Counting this flight, forty-two ma'am," (it takes forty to get a license), and with this she started in on me. "You have no business flying in here! This airport is limited to STOL aircraft (short-field takeoff and landing). You should have landed at the other airport and took a bus." Now another one of my buddies speaks up; "ma'am, do you know where we can get a copy of the ferry schedule to go home?"

After a couple of casinos and even more drinks, the guys had worked up enough nerve to get back in the plane. As we took off on the twenty-nine-hundred-foot runway, most likely still over-weight, just as a few hours ago with those red lights marking the end and water beyond, seemed to be coming up fast. I was beginning to think the plane was super glued to the runway, it didn't feel as it would ever lift off. Fixating on the red lights, I became a little anxious and pulled back on the yoke to raise the nose, but then the stall warning would go off, so I would push forward, once again observing the quickly approaching water, so again I pulled back and just as before the stall warning buzzed, I repeated this process several times. Finally, the plane wallowed into the air, no sweat we had cleared the red lights by just inches. Beyond the water was three or four-story buildings, now looking at the buildings I started this whole process over with raising and lowering the nose and the buzzer going off, again no sweat we had missed the buildings by at least a couple feet.

It is hard to describe how unbelievable it is to step from one world into an entirely different world: we had left a city and everything that comes with it, so much traffic, people in every inch of space, noisy, bright lights, glitter from the casinos, the constant background of noisy sirens, flashing lights and just generally congested all over, but now we were back in Laurel and had gotten out of the plane in the middle of the night all alone in the dark, with only the light from the rotating beacon brushing the top of the corn surrounding us, we stood there in absolute silence, other than a slight whirl noise from the beacon and the chirping cricket off in the distance. We had left a place with police and security guards everywhere, with a feeling that you could be robbed at any moment, but here I just stuck the keys under the seat along with the money that we all pitched in. It is kind of neat to think our wives and girlfriends didn't even know we left town for a few hours.

ED Young ran an aircraft maintenance shop, from time to time he would get a good deal on older planes where he would fix up and sell them. He would rent them to me, but normally pieces or parts would be missing or not working during this renovation process. He had a 1958 Cessna 172 four-seater with low air-time and a six-cylinder engine that I really liked. I was actually thinking of buying the plane. One day while working at my friend Eddie French's new house under construction, lunchtime I took his son Stevie and friend Kevin to look at this plane, then we went for a ride. We went by the new house and decided to buzz the guy still working on the job. Maybe buzz is not the right word, maybe dive bomb better describes it. To get his attention, I dove at the house, rounded out just a few feet above the driveway, even with the second-floor windows, then pulled up. We had picked up enough speed that we coasted back up to six hundred feet. Then the guy came out, so again we dove at this guy to put on a show, only this time as we rounded out the windshield burst and blew in between Kevin and me. Luckily, Stevie in the back seat was holding on to both sides for his life and was looking out the right window, so the windshield peppered the left side of his head but didn't get his face. With a strong wind in our faces and the deafening engine noise, Kevin looked at me, wanting to know what's next! I looked over and said, "I am not sure if I still want to buy this." Kevin started laughing. Stevie was still trying to decide whether to cry or scream. Landing at Laurel, I landed a little fast, thinking that no windshield could raise the stall speed. I notice that at seventy, the plane stuck to the runway like glue, at that speed it should have bounced. Normally, a plane of this age would have had the plastic windshield replaced once or twice due to sun glazing or sand pitting, but this low-time windshield was original and had turned brittle over time. I had flexed it a little more than usual. I picked up a big piece, and it broke easily in my hand. I picked up another piece and proceeded to go show Ed that we had a small problem. For a long time after that, Ed wouldn't rent me a plane, and the bank not so nicely told me that I didn't need a plane.

Now and then I would rent a plane and take my wife Kay to a nice restaurant positioned at the end of the runway in Wilmington, Delaware, named Air Squadron Command. The place was made up to look like a WWII squadron command center in England, complete with sandbag walls and broken beams in the ceiling that looked as if a bomb came crashing through; the whole place was loaded with equipment from that time, such as gun emplacements, bombs, a jeep, and even a C-47 airplane out front. It really made you feel like you were back in 1942 preparing for an air raid. The dining tables were facing a big glass window looking out over the runway and had headphones so you could listen to the air traffic. On Sundays they put on a real nice champagne brunch. One Sunday, while Kay and I were flying along in route for this breakfast, a female pilot was having trouble communicating with the tower. Maybe she thought she was on downwind but really on base or something of that sort, but the tower and she were going back and forth. You could hear the frustration building in the controller's voice. He had me holding over the oil refinery about five miles away. I just remember looking down the smokestack as I circled, when about that time he hit his limit and announced over the radio, "All other aircraft maintain radio silence until I get this woman on the ground." Having a bit of fun, I tried to get a rise out of Kay, so I went into the male chauvinist mode. "Did you hear that? That's why we shouldn't let women fly." I think I had to eat my brunch in silence.

MANY years later I returned to Atlantic City, this time with my wife, daughter, and her husband. I was now out of the construction business and now managing a pharmaceutical plant, which was the last building that I had constructed. The owners from Long Island asked me to be the plant manager. My only qualification for this position was that I was the only guy in town they knew. So, I put down my hammer and saw and started making little white pills. I had a lot to learn, first filling the place with equipment, then filling the place full of about 150 people, then actually getting product out, working 7 days a week even sometimes double shifts. For that reason, I had not been flying for quite a while; in fact, the last three entries in my logbook were biannual reviews, all in a row with no flights between. One Friday after work, I went to Georgetown, where Stew had moved his flight business, and we shot three takeoffs and landings, waited until dark and shot three more that were required for my currency. The next day we showed up around one o'clock to rent that same Warrior that I liked so much. I couldn't help but notice Stew was acting uncharacteristically all sentimental, telling his wife and mine what a great student I was, what good times we had, and so on. I thought this to be odd but didn't say anything. We took off for Atlantic City and had a smooth uneventful trip to Bader airport which was now uncontrolled. We just had a great time, bouncing up and down the Boardwalk from one casino to another. In this time before cell phones, I would stop at a pay phone occasionally and get a weather briefing. There was a strong storm system over Pittsburgh and working its way towards us, and it looked like if we left by nine o'clock, we would be okay. We were having such a good time that every time I mentioned that we needed to go, I would hear, "Just one more casino."

Finally, at midnight, the money ran out and it was time to go. I couldn't help but notice the windsock was sticking straight out if not pointing upward when we took off. Within just a couple of miles I flew straight into the stormfront with over sixty mph. wind gusts, then visibility went to zero in a blink of an eye. Once again, I was over my head; I couldn't even see the wingtips, just the glow of the green or red wingtip lights in the clouds; every time I looked away from the artificial horizon, the plane would be in at least a forty-five degree bank. I had no instrument training, I called Atlantic City Approach and stated that "I was catching weather" and could use some help. They gave me a squawk number (transponder code.) I asked Paul who was sitting in front to enter the transponder numbers like my daughter had done for me times before, but Paul threw a sh-t fit and just flipped out. So I would put a number in, look back at the artificial horizon, and the plane would be back at a forty-five plus degree bank again, then straighten out the bank. I'd put in another number, then straighten out the bank again, put in another number, straighten the bank out. "Aw hell, I forgot the last number." As I was trying to sneak a little lower so that I might be able to see, I could hear my wife and daughter saying prayers, I knew they were holding hands. When I asked the controller to return, he said, "Negative we're closed for the weather, and they couldn't help us." Then he advised me to go to Melville, that they could help me, (some thirty miles more in the storm). The controller had not been of any help all along. I was pretty sure he just wanted off the radio with me so that when we augered in, he wouldn't be on the tape when the crash was investigated. Now somewhere over Ocean City, New Jersey, I was trying to get even lower so that maybe I could see. At this point, I could make out sporadic lights and shapes as we were breaking in and out of the clouds. Looking down I could make out the handles on a trash can sitting on someone's back step, and there were red lights everywhere from radio towers. I wasted no time getting back into the clouds, then turned the plane around to what I thought was towards Atlantic City International, called the controller, and said that I was coming back. "Negative we are closed. Proceed to Melville."

I called the controller back and told him I didn't care what he said, I was coming in. Now the controller, realizing he was stuck with me, replied, "We will turn the lights up high for you." Only by the grace of God, did we break out back at Atlantic City. Still only had less than five-hundred foot ceilings, but it felt great. It is absolutely amazing how a man can go from humble as hell when he's about to die, to cover your ass mode seconds later. Now feeling safe, I asked the controller to land at Bader, knowing that nobody was there when we left, if I could get back there, maybe I would avoid getting violated, but the controller answered, "Negative. Land here." Still trying, I said, "I am more familiar with Bader," then the controller said "Negative. You land here." By this time I was just about on top of them when I was cleared to land, but the plane was at a funny angle to the runway, so I told the controller that I would have to go around. I had an easy four hundred foot ceiling at the far side of the airport, but as we returned to the approach end where the storm was coming from, the ceilings were only about hundred and fifty foot. We landed ok.

As we rolled out, the passengers regained their composure; my wife asked me if you were allowed to curse on the radio? I replied, no, why do you ask? she answered, well, you cursed. I answered, "No I didn't," then all three of them chimed in. "Yes you did." I asked, what did I say? "You told the controller, I F---ed up my approach and have to go around." I thought I had done a pretty good job of keeping my composure, covering up fears, but maybe they saw through it. Rolling out, I heard what no pilot ever wants to hear: "You need to call this phone number. Call it ASAP." I really didn't care at that moment, thinking that I might kiss the ground when this was over. I asked for progressive taxiing and we were instructed to the edge of the terminal.

Then the controller asked, "What are your intentions?" I replied we would like to park. He replied, "Negative we are closed."

I answered, it looks empty off to the left can't we park there? Once again, he replied, "Negative we are closed."

Then what do you suggest we do? He came back with, "Here is the frequencies of some of the airlines. Maybe they can help," I called one and they were accommodating, allowing us to park in their area, so we parked the little Piper Warrior between two 737s; it really looked and felt odd. Obviously pre-911 as we walked across the tarmac area leading to the buildings, trying to calm down everybody, I started explaining to my wife that this is what is meant by "weathered in." It doesn't mean I have another woman, and you really can get stuck somewhere, I explained as we walked up a wooden ramp in the back of the building leading inside. Halfway up, two of the 737 pilots wearing full uniforms came out the door. As we met, the one asked, "Where did you come from?" I answered that I got stuck in the bad weather and had to turn back. He replied, "You're lucky to be here." My wife heard that. Boy! Was that going to cost me endless headaches in my future flying days; it took me years to get her back in a plane.

Now safe inside, I found a pay phone to make that call, meanwhile my wife and daughter were carrying on. "You need to report that controller," they said. "He was arrogant and almost got us killed." Paul wasn't saying a word, in fact, he hadn't said anything since we landed. He must have blown his wad during his sh-t fit in the clouds. I told them that if I reported the controller, I'd have to report myself. When I did call, it was the controller who answered and he asked, "Are you ok? You sounded upset." I think he was just feeling me out, thinking I could make trouble.

The terminal was empty; most of the lights were turned off

and the place was really quiet, except the lone lady at the counter who appeared to be closing things up. Now about an hour past midnight, we explained that we were stuck here with no credit cards (I never take credit cards gambling, I have no discipline). The only money we had was the fifty my wife hit on the way out of the last casino. The lady was unbelievably kind. She called around and found us a cheap motel, then called a mechanic from in the back; not only did he agree to take us to a cheap motel but to pick us up the next day. The motel was what you expect for that price, run by people of foreign descent. They were nice enough, but didn't keep the place really clean. The beds and furniture were old and worn, and we saw a couple of insects crawling around. After everything else, for some reason, it didn't seem to bother us that much. Again, the airliner was more than kind, and we hung out in the pilot's lounge until two o'clock in the afternoon the next day before the weather lifted enough to go home.

A few weeks later, I called Stew's office after being humbled by this flight, wanting to start instrument lessons. As I explained to the lady that ran the office, I only wanted lessons from Stew and none of the other instructors. She answered, "Sorry he is no longer with us." I said, "What do you mean? He owns the place." She replied, "He passed away last week." A couple months later, I stopped by the place on a cold winter afternoon and found Stew's wife packing up some things. I crawled under the building to turn off the water. Mrs. Campbell showed me his logbook; it turns out I was his last student. That Saturday, as we flew off to Atlantic City, he went into the hospital with lung cancer.

BACK in my construction days, about five years before I rented Stew's plane for that infinite trip to Atlantic City, I had met a woman CEO of a large office building under construction. While trying to be a professional using, all the nickel and dime words I could come up with and not come off sounding like some country hick, I was giving her and her assistant Shawn a tour of the building site. We came upon an area built with concrete walls different from the steel stud walls and the lady asked what it was. I explained that it was where the computer mainframe and records storage room is, with special air needs and fireproof. She looked at Shawn and said, "This is where you and Joe probably will take all of your secretaries and f--- them," you could have knocked me over with a feather. I pretty much dropped all those nickel and dime words from my vocabulary after that and weeks later would fly her to Atlantic City. She would give me rolls of quarters and buy lunch. About a month after meeting them, I took Shawn up for his first flight in a small plane. As we flew along, my pager went off; the way the thing was positioned between me and the side of the seat, it was hard to tell where the noise came from. Since Shawn was known to be a bit of a prankster, I couldn't help myself and said, "Don't worry. We're just low on gas," and with that, he started to open the door! I guess the joke was on me, as I had to confess and coach him back in.

Some weeks later, he called me up and explained that his uncle had died and had been a park ranger on Assateague Island National Park. He asked would I spread the ashes over the park next Saturday? That Saturday, I had to be somewhere, so I hooked him up with another poor pilot that would love to, if they would pay the plane's rent. A day later Sunday, it was absolutely beautiful; I was doing some yard work when a plane flew over. Like so many times before, that was enough to get that flying bug, so I dropped the rake and shovel and headed to the airport. Near the end of the row of planes, I could see Stew and an assistant messing with something with a lot of fussing and cussing going on. I walked over to check this out. They had a bucket of soapy water and were scrubbing the Cessna's interior. Stew stated that some butt-hole had tried to spread ashes and didn't know that when you open the window, it creates a suction, and all the ashes came in and swirled around inside the plane, making one hell of a mess, he added the only thing that makes feel better is knowing he wore those ashes. I said that was terrible and that I never would do something like that and walked away. Still, to this day, when I think of Stew, I see that picture in my mind of him fussing and cussing, and I can't help but smile.

Chapter 2

Seven Year Itch

B eing a builder at heart doesn't necessarily mean to build with a hammer and nails. For me it can also mean to build systems a business, clubs, a new house, an education, rebuild old cars, restore old homes, or even to build the "pill plant" that I was now managing. I must feel constructive and always moving forward. For those who work outdoors or travel, what a benefit to have that change of people and scenery, for about the time one job or project gets to be the same old stuff, it's time to start a new project and meet new folks. The first several years of running the pharmaceutical plant were challenging and fascinating; I was sent just about everywhere, either for training, or to buy machinery, make deals, trade shows, even to New Orleans to consult with another company on how to construct a Class 10,000 clean room.

In recent years, some of the plant owners moved to this location from Long Island; now I had bosses on-site, the newness had worn off, growth had slowed, everything was just status quo and was running smoothly. I was no longer building a business, but just making the same old thing each day. If you made a hundred thousand pieces today, they want a hundred thousand and one tomorrow; there never seemed to be an end, never a point where the job was done. Builders need a pat on the back, "good job well done," they must have the ability to stand back and admire the finished masterpiece every so often. I longed for the days where something would break or go wrong to give me a reason for getting out of the office. Sometimes I would go out in the warehouse and just straighten up things with a forklift, but the big bosses would find out and tell me I belonged in the office. One day I had a heated argument with my boss, Partha. After we settled whatever had to be settle, Partha, who had the patience of Jobe, said to me, "You just don't work well in a structured environment, do you?" It really bothered me, because for years I stomped around that plant muttering "What do you mean I don't work well in a structured environment?" Finally, it dawned on me that maybe he was right. Some people are meant to do their own thing, to be self-employed, or own the business, I had always been the business owner, the boss. Maybe this had a little to do with wanting to get out on my own to start a crop dusting business. Thinking back, Partha always made good points, such as when President Reagan urged Gorbachev to tear down the wall, which happened when we worked together at the plant. "You know timing is everything," Partha said "If Gorbachev had tried to tear that wall down just a little sooner, he would have been standing in front of a Russian firing squad." This has always been an issue with me; a perfectly good message gets lost in bad timing or how the message is delivered, especially if the message is presented with a little too much force, as I've been known to do. Once in an awhile I'd look out the warehouse truck doors and see Rob the guy that had started flying when I did. He had recently bought out the local crop dusting business and would be in his Piper Pawnee a couple of hundred feet above the ground just scooting along in route to or from a field in the distance. Standing there thinking just how much I wanted to be up there with him, and then my thoughts would return to my present situation and I would think, (I have to get out of this place). People would ask me how long I have had this position; I would reply, I've done seven years, like a prisoner renouncing his sentence.

Rob told me where he had trained and had given me the number to the crop dusting school in Bainbridge, Georgia. They sent information and a VHS tape showing all these pilots and planes spraying crops just feet above the ground then pulling up effortlessly, turning around and diving back down; some of the footage was shot from the pilots view with country music "mister bowevel" playing in the background. The more I watched it the more I had to do this. I am not exactly sure what finally made me come home and tell my wife Kay that I wanted to become a crop duster, (to be politically correct, an aerial applicator), just like New York trash collectors like to be called sanitation engineers. This decision was not going down well with Kay.

Back in the early days of my own construction business, we poured everything we had into the business, money, time, maximum effort, even remortgaged our home to keep it going, for all this we had ended up with uncertainties, hardships, and lingering bills. Now things were going well; we could pay our bills on time, didn't have any debts, and even had a summer place in Virginia with its own sandy beach bought and paid for. From Memorial Day until Labor Day I put the plant on four ten-hour days, so all summer we had three-day weekends. Normally Kay would show up Thursday after work with the truck loaded with groceries, animals, fishing gear, etc. I would put my car in the warehouse and we would head to the beach. Real early Monday morning, she would drop me off at work, so we really had three whole days. I now had a position better than I ever thought possible with stock options, a corner office, a good salary, and a beautiful red-headed secretary. Wanting to give this up, I guess it's not hard to see why Kay and the rest of my family thought I had gone bonkers. Just the weekend before, we had gone to Virginia. I visited Windy, the crop duster near our beach home just below Cape Charles who had two Ag-Cats. He was an extremely nice guy who would give me the time of day and would tell me things about the business with some good stories. I would try to watch him fly every chance I could. The more I watched his yellow biplane with the 600 horsepower Pratt & Whitney radial engine, doing a graceful dance, just missing the trees, then turning back around in the sun and gently diving back down to just brush the tops of the plants before effortlessly pulling up for the trees at the far end of the field and turn around and start this dance all over, the more I knew this is what I wanted. To really drive the point home, that week after watching Windy, early in the morning Coreman, a Delaware aerial applicator was mosquito spraying my town, going back and forth low over our home, with a silver Beech 18, painted up with military markings. Lying in bed listing to those twin Pratt & Whitney's rumble, (nothing sounds as good as a round engine), I just couldn't stand it anymore.

Dad, if you are reading this, forgive me, but I was running out of ammunition in my battle to get Kay on board; wives just don't reason the same. So, I told Kay that my father had left my mother for another woman after eighteen years of marriage when he was about my age. His midlife crisis lasted five or six years and involved new motorcycles, cars, bars, and women, before he settled down. "Now that's in my genes, hereditary, and it is going to be hard to control. The reason that this is so important, is that I am hoping a big undertaking like crop dusting will help keep my mind off other women until I outgrow this stage of life." Kay gave in, and I would just have to be satisfied with a plane rather than another woman. She did tell me I couldn't have everything and that I would have to sell my old Packard to help pay for the school.

I sold the car to a guy in Portland Oregon. and I drove the car to Norfolk, Virginia, because his friend lived there and gave me the money and took the car. That car never ran better than that day. If it hadn't been for the fact that Kay followed me, I would have told her the guy didn't show, and kept the car. When I bought the car, it had been stored in a two-car garage next to a Studebaker; both cars were low miles. Neither had seen the light of day since 1964 when the fellow's parents passed away. For an hour after I filled the original tires with air, they popped and crackled, sounding just like a bowl of Rice Krispies, showing little cracks all over. Since I only drove the car to local shows, I never bothered to change them. The buyer, a schoolteacher, would call from time to time and ask questions like what kind of oil he should use. He planned to take his summer vacation and drive the Packard home to Portland. Later he called and said he made it; the only problem he had was he blew a tire about halfway. I asked, "Surely you didn't go cross country with tires that had been on the car since 1948?" He said there didn't seem to be a need to replace them since the tread was still good.

The guys I worked for and with at the "pill plant" were great: Dr. Potti, Ram, Suresh, Partha, Rajin, and Jag. They all put up with my good old type-A personality that could be excessive occasionally. Hindsight being what it is, I wish I would have shown more appreciation for the faith they had in me. Only after you're gone do you really know how well you had it. My bosses agreed to give me six weeks leave of absence, and I don't know why, but they paid for my new helmet. I think they sensed I was on the verge of a meltdown. With the helmet and the car money, I was off to Bainbridge for the virtually "365 days of flying weather" the school owner promised.

The small town of Bainbridge had an airport facility with a long runway, leftover from WWII when it was full of T-6 trainers during the war, but was now only slightly better than a ghost town. The dorm living quarters came with the deal; it appeared to be an old army barracks fixed up with many bedrooms, a common lounge, kitchen, and dining area nicely done for students and their spouses. The only thing that concerned me was that the bathroom had rows of toilets military style, and I thought that I might not be comfortable sitting elbow to elbow. I would get up extra early to ensure privacy, or would use the bathroom at odd times, but it turned out not to be an issue. Most of the windows were boarded up and at night it got extremely dark. When Kay came to visit, she had a panic attack; I had to go to town and buy a night-light. Evidently, right after the Oklahoma City bombing, the mechanic and a couple of the students didn't believe that fertilizer could make a bomb, so they mixed up a small amount and set it off behind the dumpster, away from everything else. Their success was much bigger than expected; luckily, nobody got hurt, the dumpster was blown to bits, but all the windows and doors were blown out of the surrounding buildings. The school's owner had all of the windows boarded up and banned all drinking on the premises.

Upon arrival, you meet the owner, sign some papers, get the low down, and pay with cash or cashier's check; you are supposed to have a commercial license and tailwheel endorsement before starting the course. I paid extra to get the commercial license there, and he agreed to do the tailwheel training as part of the Ag training. This school has had its good times and not so good times. When Rob went through things were good; things seemed to be a little tighter when I was there. Students told me that every time a new student showed up with cash, the owner would put his golf clubs in his Blanca Viking and go off and bet a thousand dollars a hole. One day as we all stood around the empty gas pump, wanting to fly, but waiting for gas that was on credit hold, I couldn't help but wonder if this is true.

Behind the maintenance building was a handful of busted up planes. One was burnt so bad that you could probably stuff it in a shopping cart. Next to it a demolish Ag-Cat with nothing left intact, which a student had brushed a tree with the spray booms on the way up, then became so preoccupied looking at the damage, he stalled out and fell back to earth with a mighty thud. Then walked two miles to a pay phone, to tell his instructor he had a problem.

In the building there were a half dozen planes in various stages of repair, among them was a Piper Comanche without an engine that I was told would be ready for my commercial instruction and check ride. There was an Ag-Cat they just bought that I was to train in, undergoing inspection. Outside was a couple of Pawnee's, an Air-Tractor, a couple of Piper Super Cubs, a handful of student personal planes, and in the back sat a Blanca Champ with a big pig head painted on the side, with the words "the pig" painted under it. The plane was missing some pieces and looked unloved. Later I found out it used to belong to my friend, Bob, and was an ex-banner plane from Ocean City Maryland.

I was lucky in getting Lance for my instructor, who was A-1; Lance looked to be in the late twenties and had been a military pilot. I was thirty-eight and older than most of the students, except Karl a truck driver and his wife, who was looking to start a new life as an ag pilot, that seemed to have stalled out working on his private pilot license. Because of the age differences and my career success, I had a tendency to be a know-it-all, which Lance put up with and tried to tame. Starting out in the Super Cubs with dual instruction, Lance would get on me, telling me I was skidding in my turns, and that I was not coordinated. Instinctively defensive, I replied that the turn coordinator gauge didn't work. He went off, saying "if you can't feel it by now, you need to go home, you don't need instruments." After that, I quit referring to the instruments, which was a good thing, since the oil pressure gauge was just about the only gauge that worked in most of these planes.

After a few weeks, I graduated from the Super Cubs and was flying solo in the Pawnees. In the morning, I could take off with ninety gallons of water, go the length of the runway, turn left, turn left again, fly upwind parallel with the runway, and when I crossed over the highway on the north end of the airport, I would have climbed to four hundred feet. In the hot afternoon I would be lucky to get a hundred feet. In this part of the training, the plane is a single seater, purposely built for the dusting business, I would fly to the designated field, and Lance would be there in his Jeep with a handheld radio to give instructions. I had progressed fairly well and was starting to feel at home spraying water. One morning I was feeling pretty full of myself; the air was cool and calm, I was having a great time pushing that Pawnee for all that it had. The whole time Lance was yelling at me on the radio, you're too low, turning too tight, and so on. I didn't pay much attention to him. I was having a good time and I just kept trying to get lower, closer, and tighter. I flew back to the airport to get the third load of water. The Air Tractor was turning downwind, and the instructor Todd was waiting next to the threshold with his handheld radio ready to talk down the student doing his first solo flight in the Air Tractor. I was coming straight in on a long final with plenty of time; for whatever reason, I just greased the landing. Todd came on the radio, "Nice landing," and after a short pause said something smart like "Must have had your eyes closed?" As I was just about to roll past him, now feeling like Chuck Yeager, I went into the invincible mode; I switched hands on the stick and with my right hand reached up and unlatched the left window, swinging it out and down, then just as I passed Todd, shot him the bird! To really get the point across, I turned around in the seat and leaned out the window, continuing to give him the bird as now he was behind me. As I turned back forward, resuming attention to the runway, the tail was just coming down, and now the plane was going left. Inadvertently I had made the plane start a left turn from turning around in the seat.

Being so full of myself, I thought I'll give them something to talk about. Since I had been there, nobody had ever landed and gotten off on the first taxiway, (about three to four hundred feet). I thought they would really think I'm hot stuff, since the plane was already heading for the taxiway; I will just let it keep on going left. The next thing I know, the plane began to spin out to the left; I hit the right break and rudder as hard as I could, no use. The plane just continued spinning around, with the tires making a terrible screeching noise. The good news and bad news is that I did end up in the taxiway, just not the way I planned. I guess all the noise got everyone's attention. About fifteen students came running towards me, and the fire company stationed on the airport rolled a truck towards me with all the lights and sirens blazing. I jumped out of the plane and noticed that the aluminum drop wingtip was bent. I quickly reached down and bent it back before the onslaught of people showed up. "Are you alright? What happened?" In the background I could hear Todd on the radio calling Lance: "You better get in here, you have a problem."

After all the initial havoc settled down, I taxied the plane back to the school, only to meet up with Lance about the same time Kay showed up; he unloaded on me. "If that's how you are going to fly, you got no business here, you never listen, you need to shut up and pay attention to what you're doing. Maybe this is not for you. Maybe you should work at Burger King instead," and he went on, and on, and on. Worst, Kay heard everything, and now it was going to be tough to get her confidence back; she would be more than happy if I would just forget the whole thing and go back to the pill plant. The students were unmerciful, there was a big marker board in the lobby that listed each student name and columns with the various steps along the training, and there was an empty column, so they wrote ground loops, "Tim 1," it served me right for acting like Mr. know-It-All. The school's owner had me busted back to the Super Cubs. The mechanic found a groove rubbed in the inboard side of the Pawnee's tire caused by the sideloading during that ground-loop, made by a brake pad bolt that was too long. They made a huge deal out of replacing the tire. Boy, how fast can a man go from totally invincible to like Isaiah sitting on a pile of cow dung, humble as hell. Tail dragger pilots say there are those that have ground-looped and those that will. I'm sure glad I got that out of the way in Bainbridge instead of around home; around pilot circles, you would always be remembered as "the guy who looped over there." Nowadays, Kay will ask, why don't you look at us or waive when you land? After all that humiliation of my lesson in Bainbridge, if Miss America were standing right next to the runway nude, I am still going to keep looking straight ahead, at least until the plane stops.

The promised "Virtually 365 days of flying," gave way to sitting around telling stories waiting for the weather to clear. Just about every three days a front would pass through, so there was a lot of hanger flying. A young British student told us about his grandfather's operation in South Africa with about forty planes; all the guys were intensely listening because his grandfather had been an ace during WWII, and they knew his name. He said that they still use tribal people to flag the fields. They would stand at the end of a row waiving a broomstick with a rag tied on top. After the plane makes a pass, the flagger would move over so many feet to mark the plane's next pass. He went on to say that occasionally the pilot would get too low and chop up the flagger with the propeller. The guys listening said, oh my god, that is terrible, what do you do? He answered, we go to the village and get another one.

The guys from South America told me that the operators down there prefer Ag-Cats because the shorter stacked wings only destroy four or five banana trees when they wreck, instead of the larger planes that may destroy fifteen to twenty trees when they crash. I gathered that pilots were more plentiful than the trees.

During the down time one of the instructors reviewing logbooks caught his student cheating on a solo cross country, who had gone about ten miles away and circled for three hours. The problem is that it should have taken four hours for the round trip. After paying my own way, in money and hardships, it is hard to imagine the young guy whose parents paid his way, and he didn't even want to be there.

As the weather cleared, I was beginning to finish the Pawnee phase, with little time left before I had to go home, it was evident that no engine was going to be put on the Comanche, and little hope of getting my money back, so I traded the commercial training for the extra tailwheel time. Part of what was chewing up my training time was that we would only get an hour here or there because of too many students for the number of planes. To get my time in, I volunteered to fly the red Pawnee that nobody wanted to fly; it had been wrecked, and something wasn't quite right. It took all varying degrees of left rudder but never any right, not even on takeoff when normally the P factor (left pull due to the propeller rotation) required right rudder.

One night after towards the end of my training the mechanic and his trainee took me out bar hopping. After we closed down the last place, they knew of another that would still be opened, so they took me down a dirt road about twenty miles.

About the time I started to get worried, we rounded the corner and there was a well-worn place (big shack) with lots of cars and music. Still, I may have had one too many; I do remember a nice-looking blond sitting on my lap, then again at that hour, all the women looked good. Then the next thing I remember was setting my alarm clock, but it was 4:30, and I had a lesson at 6:00. When Lance came knocking, I was in no condition to fly. I often wondered if I had the right stuff after witnessing these southern dusters that drink, get totally sh-t faced the night before and then jump in the plane at 5:30 the next morning like nothing ever happened. I told Lance that I had the flu and wouldn't be able to fly. With his military training, Lance didn't put up with too much bull. He made me get up; and yes, my head felt like a football. To my relief, it was raining, but he still made me help push some planes away.

I had overheard Lance one day talking with the owner, stating that he had not been paid in three months, and he was not going to instruct any more unless he got paid. I could tell that he was mentally tearing himself apart. Part of him didn't want to continue until he got paid, but another part took pride in his work and wanted to see his students through. I imagine stress is why he dumped so hard on me when I ground-looped.

When your favorite football team wins, they dump the coolers on the coach in celebration, and so goes the tradition at Bainbridge. On my last day flying the Pawnee, Lance was standing next to his Jeep watching me. I think he may have been suspicious of my motives and would not leave the side of that Jeep. The field had a crest in the middle, so I kept working the far side where he couldn't really see me; I had turned the spray down to conserve water. It took a while before Lance worked his way out in the field to see beyond the crest; finally, when I thought he was out of reach of his Jeep, I made a run on him; all I could see was the back of his white tee shirt and then his elbows switching from side to side as he ran as fast as he could. I got him with the emergency dump and almost a full tank of water. As I pulled up hard and looked back to see him face down in the mud, it was so rewarding. Back at the and airport not knowing what to expect when Lance pulled up in his Jeep soaked, before he could get a word out, I offered "Lance I am truly sorry, I'd dropped my sunglasses, and when I reached down to get them, I must have bumped the emergency dump." He calmly replied, "Yeah, I shouldn't have been there."

The next day I was killing time until the Ag-Cat was ready. I was flying the red Pawnee in one of the designated fields. I notice a flair shooting up past me. Apparently, the farmer was getting sick and tired of students buzzing around all day, every day. Needless to say, I didn't waste much time getting out of there.

With only one day left. My time was up, and I needed to get back to the pill plant. Another front with bad weather was coming and was expected to last for many days. They got the Ag Cat out; finally, I would get a chance to fly the plane of my dreams. Checking me out took a little while. Constant speed props and the position of the controls were new to me. With a puff of smoke, the engine came to life with that deep throat rumble only a radial engine makes; I was excited as this was everything I had ever wanted. After warming it up for fifteen minutes, it was time to taxi out and make this dream come true. As I went to turn, the right brake pedal went to the floor. It was nice while it lasted. They would not have the plane fixed before the weather came in. Lance had let his conscience win his moral dilemma and saw me through to the end; he did all he could and more, and now he left for home. With a Certificate of Completion suitable for framing in hand, along with an IOU for five hours of Ag Cat time, but out of time and money, Kay and I got in the car and headed home to Salisbury.

Chapter 3
Back In Town

N ow back home and back to work at the pill plant, I was still in need of a commercial license. Easton airport had a Beechcraft Sierra, so after work and on weekends, I would take lessons. It was tough. I was pulling long hours at the pill plant, because I felt it necessary to make up for the paid leave of absence I was given for Bainbridge. With Robert, a college student, working for the Easton's FBO as my instructor, I managed to make progress. Sometimes after a lesson Robert would reach under the panel and pull the wire to the Hobbs meter that kept track of the hours that you paid rent on, and we would clown around doing rolls and loops, and I would simulate crop dusting runs.

One night after having a lesson followed by some clowning around, I advised Robert that maybe we should quit screwing around, since I noticed that the door was rubbing the wing when we opened it, and it didn't rub before our flight.

Preparing me for the check-ride, Robert advised me this is an easy check-ride, you are expected to be a professional, and don't waste too much time trying to memorize everything, if the examiner has you do any calculations, write down all the numbers past the decimal point to show preciseness. Then he added "The answer to most questions is refer to the checklist.

Mr. Crescent was my examiner; and the first thing he asked was to make a flight plan from here to Savanna, Georgia. I slaved away, putting all the numbers past the decimal, adjusting fuel burn for climbs, adjusting for pressure, adjusting for crosswinds, and more on each leg. While working on the third page of figures, he got tired of waiting and wanted to see what I already had. He said, "Good grief man, I just wanted to know if we had enough gas." In the plane doing lazy 8s, he reached over and pulled the power; I immediately set up for a landing in the adjacent bean field. As we passed through eight hundred feet, he responded with a stern voice, "Don't you have a checklist?" I replied, "you don't have time for that crap. This thing drops like a brick." Mr. Crescent told me, "That's the wrong answer!" But he went on to say, "but you are right, I am sick and tired of all these young guys that think they are going to get out the checklist and read half a book before they plow dirt." Satisfied with emergency procedures, we moved on to shooting landings, on the downwind nearing the base turn he asked, "Does that airspeed gauge adjust for true airspeed?" The gauge was on the far left, so I reached over and gave a half-ass try to turn the glass face and told him, (not wishing to fool with it) "No, it's stuck." "Let me try," he said, and he reached across me to turn it, but it still wouldn't turn. Next thing I know, he's got both arms reaching across, with a good bit of his 350 lb. body in my lap. Finally, I said, "Good grief man, you're just supposed to drop a pencil and ask me to pick it up or something of that sort for the distraction part of this test." He just laughed, and with that I rode home with a commercial license in hand, feeling that now I might just make it.

NOW it was time to become the "Whore of the Airways," up to this point I had paid for every hour that I logged, but now so I could build hours I would fly anyone anywhere, for anything, if they would just pay for the plane rent. Even though I had a paper in my pocket that said I was a qualified commercial pilot, and even after all the 3s that I turned to 8s in my logbook to have enough hours to get this far, employment was many hours away. I would take Realtors up to get photographs for their advertisements, golfers to North Carolina, friends to Atlantic City, and anybody else that would chip in. I started bugging the ag operators hoping to land a job. Rob would entertain the idea, but said he had three fully experienced pilots waiting already, Windy, Carter, and Baggett all were one-man shows didn't need help, Coreman had plenty of pilots already, and Al Johnson just came right out and said, "There must have been a hundred of you guys looking for a job already," and sent me away.

SOMEONE told me there was a crop duster named Dave between Felton and Sandtown about forty miles away. Riding around the back roads, I found the hanger with an Air-Tractor parked out front, but I could find nobody around, but in the field next to the runway was a man hoeing watermelons, and a woman farther down the field also hoeing. I walked across the field to inquire about the plane's owner; it turned out that he was the owner and he had planted the melons mostly for his girlfriend to make a little extra money. Dave also went on to explain that they had a fight the previous night and weren't speaking; he didn't know if she was going to move out. I advised him to just break the ice and talk to her, and he said he was thinking about it if they met up at the end of the row. He told me he wished he had met me last year as he had just taken on a new partner. So, this is how I met Dave, who would turn into a good friend, and from time to time will pop up in my stories.

SATURDAY, a week after meeting Dave, outside Berlin, Maryland, I met another guy that would turn out to be a good friend, Bob was the owner of the Ocean City banner planes. He employed six to eight pilots pulling banners, and they also gave biplane rides along the beach. In addition Bob did some crop dusting himself. It was an overcast, misty day, we talked in the middle of a dark hanger filled with a dozen planes of all shapes and sizes that were packed in there tight like a jigsaw puzzle. Over in the corner two guys were tinkering with the left wingtip of a shiny red biplane. As we were talking an older fellow walked up to us. Bob turned his attention to him and said, "How do you feel about it now?" The fellow replied, "I think I got the hang of it now." Then Bob said, "It's too windy now, come back tomorrow." Then the guy left. Bob turned his attention back to me and said the fellow had ground-looped the plane earlier, and that was what the two guys were fixing. Sensing a chance, I started in on Bob. "Why don't you hire me? I just returned from a school where the only thing we fly is tailwheel." Bob informed me that I didn't have enough hours and that the older guy was a 747 pilot with thirty thousand hours, and that's what the insurance company wanted. Sunday evening, as Kay and I were having dinner and watching the six o'clock news, they flashed a picture of that shiny red biplane headfirst in a ditch with the tail sticking straight up in the air. I am thinking the older fellow "didn't get the hang of it."

Although most operators will tell you to come back for a job when you have a least five hundred hours, some will insist on a thousand hours. Hours are important, but sometimes just a warm body will do if you are in the right place at the right time. Ramiro owned a banner business serving the Rehoboth, Delaware area. I showed up at his grass strip the day after Labor Day. All the banner tow pilots had left for the season. Desperate for a pilot, he said he would give me a try, but said it would take two or three days to train. Friday after work I met with Ramiro to start my training, and he introduced me to Carl the ground crew. On the edge of the runway sat an old rusty wrecked oil truck that looked as if it had had a head-on crash with a cement truck, Ramiro climbed on top and opened a big round hatch. "Now this is how you gas up," he said with a lit cigarette hanging from his lips. He picked up a 12-volt fuel pump with about eight foot of pipe attached to the bottom and 50 foot of black hose hooked to the side and slid it down into the blue aviation gas. I wanted to run like hell, fearing an explosion, but I took my chances that he had gotten away with this many times before. Then he climbed down and hooked the cables to Carl's truck battery.

After we gassed up the Cessna 150 with a 150 horsepower engine, Ramiro wanted to check out my flying. First, he asked me to hold straight and level for a couple of minutes while I turned around and looked out the back window, because he said, I would spend a lot of time looking back. Next, we flew the beach from Rehoboth to Lewes with him pointing out where I was to start and end the run up the beach and the best positioning for people to read the banner. We flew back to the country strip, where I threw a hook out the window. Then I was supposed to fly through the poles with the hook dangling on 15 feet of rope attached to the tail of the plane and try to snag a piece of rope that is stretched between two plastic poles about six feet high and six feet apart, with that dangling hook. Later, the piece of rope would be hooked to a banner. Before I even got to try, Ramiro looked at his watch and said, "I'm late for a party, come back tomorrow, and we'll train some more," so we knocked off.

Saturday morning, I showed up, Ramiro wasn't there, only Carl. Carl told me, "Ramiro had to fly for Executive Jet today, and he said you would be ok." He gave me a note from Ramiro, that said "Tim, remember in the beginning two out of three times you will probably miss picking up. Just take your time and don't get flustered," and then there was a list of fourteen banners to tow. At the bottom was another instruction telling me if a banner doesn't release when you go to drop it, don't land with it on the grass, the banner may get snagged and flip the plane, so land with it at Ocean City airport on the pavement so it will slide, Georgetown doesn't allow banners. Beginners luck I guess, but I never missed a pick-up. Carl told me that around lunchtime Ramiro had called, and he had told Ramiro that I was fantastic. Of course, this went right to my head, as I thought nobody has had a perfect first day, they'll think I'm hot stuff. But just like the game kids play, if you're the king of the hill, there is only one place to go: Down! The very last banner I missed the pick up. Now irritated that I blew that perfect record, I went around and missed again; now I was livid. As I do occasionally, I talked to myself. I can remember saying "I'll get that s.o.b. this time," and flew right through the poles and pulled up (all day I had pulled banners made with stuck together letters, but this last one was a big Budweiser panel job with a ton of drag). As I rounded out on the top of the pull-up, the rope took up hard, throwing me forward into the instrument panel. For a moment I thought the plane had just quit moving. At the same time Carl's voice came over the radio, "You got it," which he always says when I would hook one. While pushing the nose over even more, I answered, "Yes I know! What the hell, did you tie it to a tree?" Then he called back." No, you hooked it with your wheels, Ramiro says you have to take it to Ocean City." I said, "it's not going to fall off. I may's well haul it down the beach first and complete our list. Carl put up some argument that I had to go to OC right then, but since I wanted to complete all of the day's work, I outvoted Carl. Labor Day weekend just the week before, Bob's replacement pilot for the 747 pilot that had wrecked the biplane had a terrible accident, and the media wouldn't let it go; anything and everything having to do with aircraft was news. Fearing that I could make the news with an overstated "emergency landing," I called Carl back and instructed him that when he drove to the airport to pick up the banner, not to tell anybody what we were doing. That banner had to be hauled from 90th St. OC to Rehoboth twice. It took an hour and a half, and when heading for OC airport, I called in for the wind. The radio answered," Sky Banners is that you? We've been waiting for you,"(thanks Carl). I came across the threshold about three hundred feet, goosed the power for couple seconds to get the banner to rise, chopped the power and pointed the plane straight at the ground. At the last second, I pulled the flaps and rounded out just a couple feet above the runway. Poof, that was it. The plane probably didn't even roll out fifty feet. I turned around just in time to see the banner float down to the runway. I climbed out of the plane with the engine still running, and unhooked the rope. Carl rolled up the banner and threw it in the back of his pickup. I got in the plane and hauled ass before anybody came. The way I see it, thirteen out of fourteen is pretty good for having never picked up a banner ever before. Hell if it were your favorite football team, that score would get them in the playoffs.

The next day I towed seven more banners, and some guy named Paul came and towed three or four. We were so busy towing, I never got to meet him. Around two o'clock, I notice some smoke in the direction of the airstrip; as I flew closer, I could see all kinds of blinking lights. As I got even nearer, I could make out a half-dozen fire trucks to go with the blinking lights. The end of the runway was all black and burnt up. After I landed, a guy from the power company came over and fussed me out. "I told them to have those wires moved, but they're too cheap," and he went on to say this was the third time. I just answered "Yes sir, I am really sorry." He was so wrung up, I didn't see much point in explaining it wasn't me and I was just the new guy and didn't know what in the hell he was talking about. Apparently, a little while before I came back from the beach, Paul had drugged his banner through the power lines near the end of the runway on the way in and all the sparks set the field on fire.

Since it was off-season, only a handful of banners had to be towed every Saturday. I hadn't seen Ramiro since that first Friday night, and Carl only came if there were several banners to do. Most of the time I was on my own. Normally, I had to stick the rolled-up banner in the passenger window going towards the back with part of it hanging out, fly to the banner airstrip, roll out the banner, hang the rope in the top of the poles, and gas up myself. Gassing up was a job all by itself. I had to climb up on the decrepit tank truck, open the hatch, put the pump in, climb down with the long battery cables, then climb behind the seats of the small Cessna, crawl through the back hatch towards the tail where the battery is, then hook up the cables. When I would get halfway back, the plane would come off the front wheel and tilt up; then I had to climb backward uphill until the plane tilted forward again to get out. After gassing up, I had to repeat this process all over again to unhook the pump.

In their wisdom, the county council had approved Ramiro's grass runway in the middle of a big farm field which Ramiro rented from the farmer; however, we were not allowed to leave planes there overnight, so every morning I would go to George's house were the planes were kept. He had a short narrow runway with trees on one end and a mobile home on the other, and corn planted tight to the runway. It was about twenty miles away from the banner field. Every morning I would strap my Dunkin' Donuts coffee under the passenger seatbelt. Halfway to the strip, I would try a barrel roll, and every time while inverted, the plane would fall out and head straight for the ground. So one day, I got the brilliant idea that if I pushed in on the yoke when the plane was upside down, that the plane would stay up. When I pushed forward, maybe a little too hard or something, with the negative Gs, the steel tow bar behind the seats came up and smacked me in the back of the head, (liked to knock me out), and coffee went flying everywhere, all over the ceiling, windshield, seats, panel, and me. It was a couple weeks before I'd try that again.

After Halloween, I towed banners around the pumpkin chunking contest where they shoot, throw or fling pumpkins to see how far they will go. By now the winner was shooting a pumpkin thousands of feet. Trying to do an outstanding job, I was a little lower than normal when a pumpkin came flying up, pass the left wing. It didn't take me long to get back up to where I should have been. The next week, along with Paul, I towed banners around the Dover NASCAR race. I had the Larry's Mobile Homes banner, and Paul had some pizza joint. I went around the racetrack at about six hundred feet, and Paul went around at about a thousand feet. Vicky, Ramiro's wife, kept sending messages that the pizza owner wanted his banner lower, to be towed like the Larry' Homes, once again swelling my head. After a while, I saw Paul's plane over the town, and then he starts dropping. It looked as if he was going to hit the Capital dome. I called on the radio; "Paul pull up, pull up." It turned out that he had been fiddling with the mixture knob when it fell apart in his hand and was having a hard time getting the mixture back on. After that day I never saw Paul again.

It was Valentine's Day morning, colder than crap, when I showed up at George's to haul a personal banner (like will you marry me); it had to be done by eleven o'clock. The planes were frozen and hadn't been used for a while, and I tried to jump all four planes with my car battery; the only one that I could get started had very little gas, it wasn't enough gas to get to the Rehoboth strip. With no gas at George's, the only thing I could do was to drain the gas out of one of the planes that wouldn't start into a two-gallon can and pour it in the plane that would run; meanwhile, Vicky kept calling to check my progress. After all of my heroics, eleven o'clock came and went, and they canceled the banner. Frustrated by this, I stopped by Bob's in Berlin that I had met earlier trying to get a job. Since I now had some experience towing banners and I had bought my own Ag-Cat, he was more willing to talk with me about a job.

Chapter 4
My New Old Plane

When I was in my early 20s and still single, on lunch break a co-worker was telling me his older married brother wanted to buy a duck hunting boat and his wife wouldn't let him. The next Saturday morning I went to visit a friend, as usual he was still in bed. While I was waiting for him to get going, I sat at the dining room table and his father handed me a cup of coffee. This had become routine, so I gotten to know the father well. I notice this guy had been able to attain many different things like a boat and motorcycle without much resistance from the wife. Because I was contemplating marriage, but concerned that I might not be able to have anything like a duck boat, so I asked him how he was able to acquire these toys with the wife being agreeable. He said "You must have a plan. For example, sometime ago I had taken up golf and knew I wanted to buy an expensive set of golf clubs. So, I bought a cheap set at a yard sale and after a while I told the wife that they were worn and didn't work well, she agreed to let me trade them in on the expensive ones. Had I tried to get the expensive clubs first she would have thrown a flag on the play."

After talking to my friend's father and thinking about the co-worker's brother, I decided to acquire a few things of my own, such as a motorcycle and a couple more rusty collector cars. A couple of the old rusty cars were absolutely piles of junk with very little possibilities of being restored. Knowing that later on if I already had that old dusty rusty toy sitting in the corner, there is a good chance of negotiating a trade-in or upgrade. I did notice that before marriage women are more agreeable to helping their man buy some kind of toy, but after marriage all bets are off. This strategy worked well for me, one car for the ag school and another car for a plane. If you wait until after the wife and kids come along to get that toy, you could find yourself entered in unpleasant conversations, getting the silent treatment, divorce court, or at the least, you may have to buy some gold jewelry to offset your purchase.

From time to time, I would call my father, who had a new Heritage Special Harley Davidson, and say "Let's go riding." Often he would say his bike was in the shop, and I would say, "Why don't you get one of these Hondas. It never breaks down, it's quiet, and my maintenance program consists of running a garden hose over it in the springtime." He would answer me, "You're probably right, but it's not a Harley." One night I called my father and told him that I was getting ready to buy my first plane. I had found an older Piper Pawnee through the Trade-A-Plane newspaper. I explained how it was one of the smaller dusting planes and would burn less gas than some of the others, maintenance would be manageable, it was lower-priced and since I didn't know if I would even get 5 cents worth of business, it seemed sensible. Sensing that I was searching for answers, my father said, "But what?" I answered, well, I always wanted a bi-plane with a round engine, but it burns a lot more gas, not many guys will work on them anymore, also it cost a good bit more, and since I don't know how much business I'll get, I could end up starving. With that he replied, "Yeah, it's just not a Harley, is it?" After I hung up, I made arrangements to buy the round en-gine biplane (the Harley Davidson of the airways). Remember my advice: for the record, this time I had to part with another old car to get the plane, just to keep the wife happy.

THE day finally came that I was to get my first airplane, a 1963 Grumman Ag-Cat. I packed some charts, a new handy dandy electronic flight calculator, a change of clothes, a cashier's check, and all the cash I had in the world, just about $900. I went to work early Thursday morning, got all the troops straight and told them I'd be back Monday, then talked my co-worker and friend Kris into driving me to the local airport. We had plenty of time, I was worried about flying home with no radio, so at the last minute, I called Ramiro and asked to borrow his handheld radio.

We rushed what was thought to be about 15 minutes away, but it turned out to be more like 35 minutes to get the radio. Now pushed for time we drove to The Salisbury airport as fast as Kris's VW diesel Rabbit would go, then I ran into the terminal, I could see one engine turning on the commuter plane, but the other engine hadn't started yet. I tried to talk my way on, waving my tickets, but to no avail. After they examine my tickets, I was advised that with the layover time to my next flight, if I hurried, I could make the BWI connection.

As we rushed to the car, Kris threw me the keys and said,

"You drive, I know you're in a hurry, and I don't want a ticket." Sure as hell, 45 miles later coming off the Cambridge bridge, I got stopped for speeding. When I climbed back in the car, exasperated, I threw the wallet down on the floorboard with a little fussing and cursing. We continued on, driving as fast as I thought I could get away with, to BWI. We pulled up to the terminal, and I ran to the counter once again waving my tickets, only to be advised that I was too late. Being helpful, they told us that if I rushed, I could trade in the tickets to Atlanta, Georgia at Washington National and make the next flight, so off we went. Hallelujah, we made it! Wouldn't you know it, as I was boarding, they wanted my ID. This is when it becomes apparent that my wallet was on the floorboard of Kris's car with no chance of getting it now.

Being pre 9/11 days, I was able to talk my way on, showing my pilot license. Mostly I think they let me on because they didn't want to see a grown man cry. Once on the plane, it sat on the tarmac for a half hour or more because of passing storms at the next stop Atlanta, Georgia. You guessed it! Too late for the connection! No sweat, they traded my tickets for a later flight.

Finally, I made it to Shreveport, Louisiana after 10 pm., and the place was pretty much empty with most of the lights off. Only one person at the counter, and a note on the desk from the seller: "Too late, get up with you tomorrow." I got on a van with the flight crew to a hotel, the hotel didn't want to give me a room because I wanted to pay cash, and had no ID. Here we go again with the wallet situation. I was hoping this day is not an omen of what's to come. Luckily the pilot stepped in and said he's with us.

The next morning it was overcast with a light drizzle. I met

Scotty, the seller, who seemed like a decent guy, in his mid-40s and average shape, not overbearing in the least, but you could tell that he knew the business and had it going on. We had breakfast and then he drove me about 30-40 miles to his airstrip and shop. As we turned in, I could see a lone Ag-Cat with nothing else around it sitting on the back edge of a fair-sized cement pad. It looked like a red-headed stepchild that nobody wanted, all alone, shivering in the cold rain, chained down to the cement pad with chains big enough to hold a tugboat. "There she is," Scotty proclaimed. I can't really say I was elated nor disappointed. It just wasn't the sexy looking plane that I envisioned, but on the other hand, I hadn't paid too much either. We made the deal. It rained and turned cold, and the mud puddles froze at night which surprised me for being in the south, and stayed that way for several days, but then again it was the week before Thanksgiving. I hung out in the shop, to a city boy in the pharmaceutical business dreaming of being a duster; it was just amazing. He had two 802 Air Tractors, the biggest they make. Scotty explained how they work, how he flies and what he does, including night spraying, then he let me sit in one. Wow! Then he showed me where Dennis, the head pilot and a mechanic, was installing a turbine wheel, it was about the size of a 45 record. Then he picked it up off the bench and handed it to me to see. As we talked, I nonchalantly began to kind of thump it against my other hand. As I asked some questions, I could see the color was leaving Scotty's face, then he explained that thing that I was thumping cost about sixty thousand. So very carefully, I set it down.

The weather stayed the same for the next couple of days. Meanwhile, Dennis showed me some things about my plane but didn't explain much about how things worked, as I may have misled them about my experience. He shared some stories, like when warming up the airplane in the morning, be sure that you wait for the engine to quit speeding up as it warms up before you get out to use the bathroom, because you may find yourself running out of the bathroom, pulling up your pants trying to catch the empty plane speeding away. How short our memories are. I more or less repeated that story one cold morning, one time a few years later, running out of the bathroom chasing a plane with the slowly speeding up engine heading for the corn field! One night Scotty took me to the local watering hole; over a few drinks, he explained that he really didn't know a lot about my plane. He had mostly flown Air Tractors but had just purchased the plane from an old family friend as a favor and let newer pilots practice with it before allowing them to fly his more expensive airplanes.

The next morning, still overcast and cold but a good 500-600 foot ceilings I was ready to go home. The night before, I had laid out all the charts on the hotel floor, carefully lining up all five chart edges, to show my cross country trip home. With about 8 feet of string, I made a straight line, and with a marker I traced a line on the charts home across 7 states. Now all I had to do was figure fuel stops with my new handy dandy electronic pathfinder flight computer, find out how big the gas tank was and what the fuel burn was from Scotty. That morning, I asked Scotty how big the gas tank was; he wasn't sure. He and Dennis agreed that the Ag-Cat center tank was 46 gallon and should burn about 19-20 gallons an hour. So I punched it in the pathfinder and came up with the next couple of stops. I stuck all my stuff in a trash bag and hung the bag in the chemical hopper, which didn't smell too good. With charts in hand, I climbed up and in the plane while Scotty stood next to it. He asked me, " Have you ever flown one of these?" I replied, " Oh yeah. Lots of times." Then he asked me, "do you want some earplugs?" I replied, "No thanks," then he asked, "Do you want some gloves?" And then the old construction worker slipped out, so I replied, "Only p-ssys wear gloves." And with that, I told him that I would like to do a couple of landings here before going home. He said, "Ok, although we haven't used the paved runway for years because of all the potholes, we just use the grass next to the runway. But since all this rain flooded the grass, use the paved runway and just try and miss the potholes." I replied, "No problem," and with this I proceeded to get the plane started and warmed up.

Once the plane was ready, I taxied to the end of the runway, now I was proud of myself that I had smoothly started the plane. The thing with me is that I can go from apprehensive to overconfident in a flash, so with no further thought, I jammed the throttle forward, and the plane responded immediately. I had only flown a Cessna 150 recently and had minimal tailwheel experience. As the plane began to take off, I began to lecture myself, "Don't forget you're in a tail dragger and have to push forward on the stick to get the tail up first!" As I was trying to figure out when to push forward on the stick, I looked out the window and saw that I was already about 30 feet off the ground. Shoo! I don't have to worry about that anymore, and one thing for sure, I will return to the ground somehow. After a few simulated crop dusting passes on the adjoining field, it was time to try to land. I noticed the airspeed gauge didn't work. Without the earplugs that had been offered, the engine was deafening. I adjusted the throttle, which was rusty and really hard to push, it almost took two hands to move. Reliant only on the engine sound, and just the feel of the plane I tried to set up the landing speed.

I crossed over the power lines at the end of the runway near where Scotty was standing. I had a nice, smooth, steady sink going, and felt good, but as the ground was coming up quick, it dawned on me, I had been judging my speed by the engine noise and had gotten too slow, I thought I better put some power in to arrest the sink. Being too slow to respond coupled with an engine that takes what seems like a lifetime to come back to life, the engine kicked in just about the same time the plane bounced for the first time. As I bounced back into the sky, I chopped the power only to reapply power before the next bounce and so on, each bounce getting a little smaller until it came to rest at the end of the runway. It would have been no problem to fit a small house under the first bounce, and I suppose this is what they call pilot-induced oscillations. Even after all the early silent films that I have seen like Laurel and Hardy, and the Keystone cops, where planes crash into barns and through buildings, most would agree this was even more ugly. Things never really come easy for me, so it's just normal to get back on the horse after being thrown, except I believe that you have to slug the horse in the head first before getting back on. So with that, I taxied back to the starting point, determined not to let that plane kick my butt. When I got down there, Scotty was profusely waving his arms STOP, STOP! It was evident that he figured out that maybe I was not a hundred percent truthful about flying this kind of plane, "lots of times."

As I climbed out, Scotty advised me that maybe I would be better off to practice landings at my next stop, a nice big county airport with lots of room. What else can you do in this situation? So I just looked him square in the eye and said, "What's wrong? Are you afraid that you may end up on the six o'clock news?" Then I think he became concerned about my plight; after some more advice, he brought out a handheld GPS. They were pretty new and expensive at that time, and I had never seen one except in the magazines. He showed me how to work it and offered to let me use it for my trip home and said to just mail it back. This time it was for real and I climbed back in. The next stop was about 180 miles, and I would just hold a heading about 70 degrees all the way home. When I took off the left window popped open, as it had on the first flight. It was a distraction at a bad time, just when I was trying to concentrate on landing or taking off. Once I got leveled off and turned in the general direction, I tried to pull the window shut, but it took both arms to close it. Every time the power setting was changed, the window would pop open, which was a real pain. For one it was cold, also the trim was designed for having a load, so it wouldn't trim down, no matter what. When I would let go, the plane would shoot straight up, so you had to try and hold the stick with your knees, while at the same time lean out the left window with both arms to close it. I wasn't smart enough to know to slip the plane and allow the window to almost close itself. Scotty's GPS worked great, thank God, because every time I messed with the charts and let go of the stick, the plane would shoot straight up, and with only 500 foot ceilings, this put me in the soup. Going IFR is not good when the only working instrument is an oil pressure gauge. Somehow I made the airport okay and, much to my surprise, not too bad of a landing. I was freezing, but had learned a lot! So I borrowed the airports' curtesy car, went to

Walmart, bought gloves, a hat, earplugs, socks that had batteries and heat, channel lock pliers, and bungee straps to hold the window shut.

The next stop was about the same distance, and I felt more comfortable with the plane. GPS was a big help since I couldn't get much more than 4 to 5 hundred feet; at that altitude can be difficult to get the overall picture. It is a lot easier to navigate at higher altitudes; the land features such as rivers, lakes, hills, towns, roads and power plants, will look much as depicted on the charts. On the charts, the water is blue, and the land is brown. Because of all the rain, almost everything looked like water under me, and in the Delta area, it all looked the same, with no good landmarks; this made me rely more on the GPS and less on the charts. It was still frigid, and the more I relaxed, the colder it seemed. The plane had air holes everywhere, so I began to rip off the chart's bottom and stuff pieces in the air holes. Things were going well when the GPS screen faded to blank. I suppose it blanked out because it was one of the early models using liquid-crystal like my old Casio watch. If you ever left one out in your cold car overnight, it would be blank, but when it warmed up, the numbers would reappear, so I began to rub it, to no avail, so I placed it between my legs hoping to warm it, but nothing worked. As I fumbled with it, it slipped and fell to the belly of the plane, with no chance of retrieving it. This plane is built with a steel tube framework, where your feet rest is about a foot and half above the belly. The GPS landed face up and the screen lit up, just to tease me, with no chance of getting it back.

In situations like this, I find it helps if you talk to yourself: (so I began, stay cool, keep a heading about 70 degrees, and things will be fine). After a while, nothing out the window looked anything like the chart; I know I crossed the mighty Mississippi river, and where I crossed had a lot of bends in the river, but none looked like the bends shown on the chart, so I had no idea how far north or south I was when I crossed. It seemed like a longer time than it should have. Now I wondered if the part of the chart I needed was ripped off and jammed in around the windshield. The gas gauge hung under the top wing at the top of my vision when I looked straight ahead. It worked like a clock face, with the 4 o'clock position being full, then it turned counterclockwise to the 6 o'clock position being empty, and it was pointing at about 9 o'clock. With the thought of being lost and the fuel going down, I began to get a little uptight, so (I kept telling myself hold 70 degrees, and everything will be ok). After a while, I came upon an airport; simultaneously, I could see a big lake ahead on the right. The chart with the line that I had drawn the night before showed a lake with a dam about ten miles before my destination, and if you drew a straight line off the dam, it pointed right to the airport. Looking ahead of the lake and dam, I could see a blinking light that looked about ten miles beyond. Instead of being sensible and landing at the airport almost under me and ask where am I, so I headed for the blinking light. As I approached the light, it was just a radio tower with no airport in sight. By now, the gas gauge was pointing at seven o'clock and seemed to be moving down faster and faster. I turned back for the perfectly good airport that I passed, calling myself a dumbass and every name I could think of. The funny thing about the placement of that fuel gauge is you can't not look at it if you don't want to look anymore. By now, it hit the six o'clock empty position. While looking ahead in search of that airport, I had noticed a black fuel line coming down the left strut from the fuel tank in front of me. By now, I was sweating, and all sudden, I wasn't cold anymore. I put the plane in a slight slip to keep the left lower so what fuel was left would go towards that fuel line (later, when I wasn't so nervous, I notice there was four fuel lines coming out of the tank with one on each corner. Slipping the plane was just a waste). Just as I approached the middle of the airport, the engine sputtered about three times and quit. To my amazement I really wasn't worried anymore and thought (when the engine quit it really did sound like the ones in the movies). It looked like I had it made, I thought I even had time for somewhat of a proper pattern. Boy was I wrong, that plane really came out of the sky quick! Now forgetting the pattern, I was just trying to make the airport. I would have to T-bone the runway, for a minute it didn't look as if I would clear the trees, then the fence and lastly clear the rocks beyond the fence, but by the grace of God I made it to the grass edge of the runway. It's funny how your brain can go from normal to emergency mode and back again just that quick. Instead of being thankful that I beat the odds and glad to be alive, I immediately went into cover your ass mode and decided if I could only get onto the runway, I wouldn't risk getting a violation. As the plane rolled out, heading at the runway, the edge of the runway pavement was about 6 inches above the grass; when the engine quit the prop had stopped straight up and down. The plane was still moving pretty fast. I applied breaks to not to overshoot the far side of the runway. Well, between the small wheels, long prop straight up and down, the concrete's edge, and breaking with the tail up, it happened! I had struck the prop on the concrete and bent it, and God knows where in the hell I am, and I couldn't even get off the runway.

It turned out I was in Batesville, Mississippi, quite away from the Farmingdale, Alabama, that I was shooting for. The lady at the airport office called a guy from the next building to help get the plane back up front. We gassed it up; it took almost 32 gallons not the 46 gallons that I was told that it held; later, I found out that early Ag-Cats had 33 gallon tanks standard, this helps explain why I ran out since I had entered 46 gallons in the handy dandy flight computer. After considering my options, I pulled out the channel lock pliers and was attempting to bend the propeller blade back. Only the last 3 or 4 inches was bent. Some man came over from the shop across the way and asked, "What are you doing?" I replied, "I've bent this, and I need to get back home to Delaware."

"You can't do that," he said. I replied, "Sure I can. Do you have any bigger pliers?" With that, he gave a stern look. He told me that even if you did get that bent back, there was a good chance under load it would crack and break off. Worst yet, with just one blade bent, the unbalance would shake me to pieces. Before you could chop the power, most likely, the engine would vibrate off the mounts, then the plane would come back down to earth tail first and I wouldn't survive. Then he added "If you go ahead and do it, I'll call you in."

Stuck at a strange airport with a damaged plane that pretty much kicked my butt, and a guy that wanted to call me in. I had emptied out my bank account buying the plane, now with no wallet, and most of the money I brought for the trip gone do to all the extra days waiting for the rain to stop in Louisiana, and I was supposed to be back at work last Monday. Now it's Friday afternoon. How much can a man take? I was strongly considering prying off the metal tag on the plane with the serial number, leave the plane and take a Greyhound bus home, forget the whole damn thing.

My parents are just old enough that they spent their formative years during the Great Depression, as opposed to many of my friends parents that came of age after WWII; it seemed that my parents were stricter, with good old fashion values, like hold the door for ladies, never wear a hat inside, a man's word was enough, give an honest day's work, grown men don't need or accept help, own up to responsibility, never take handouts. It would be disgraceful ever to accept public assistance, the family would strongly disapprove. For these reasons, this was the low point of my life; a full-grown man at age 38, I would have to call my mom for help.

Not sure, but I think the lady at the office called a guy a couple of buildings down, asked him to see if he could help out this poor lost guy with a broken plane. I met Randy, he listened to my story and said, "Let's see if we can't fix it." It turns out that Randy and his partner Jim were in the dusting business. In their hanger sat two planes, one was a turbine Thrush, pretty big and looked to be shiny new, the other was a turbine Ag-Cat. How cool! From the front it had a big shiny spinner, and with about 6-inch shiny exhaust coming out both sides pointing towards the back. For a guy like me, it was like standing in front of a beautiful Ferrari. However, from the side view, the extended front looked like a plane with Jimmy Durante's nose stuck on the front. Randy, rooting through things in the corner, said he thought he had a prop that would work, but after checking it out, the hub was for a different size engine. Randy took me into the office, nice with a couple of desks, a computer, copiers, and a waiting area with a refrigerator, couch, easy chairs, TV and coffee table. Back at his desk, he looked through the rolodex for numbers of prop shops. Being late in the day, no one answered. We tried ads from trade magazines: no answers. It looked like I would have to wait until Monday morning, Randy said. With that, he loaned me a company car, gave me directions to a cheap motel, gave me a key to the office, and told me that I could hang out there until things straighten out. Wow!

That night in the motel room, I turned on the GPS; now that the screen decided to work and reappeared still showing the dotted line (my flight path). It showed I was holding about 70 degrees, then about halfway to the next airport turning pretty much straight north for quite a ways, until seeing all the funny business, where I had traveled by the lake and towers, and back to the Batesville airport. It was clear that along with most of the other gauges, the compass didn't work either. After checking the GPS out, I called my wife and once again explained I wouldn't be home right away, then called Mom to ask for her credit card.

The weekend seemed to drag on forever, still cold and since it was off-season almost nobody was at the airport. Finally, Monday rolled around and Randy showed up. After a few calls and being told they did not have what I needed or they couldn't fix it, Randy hooked me up with Chester from Chester Roberts Supply in Texas. Chester had a prop, and more importantly, knowing the pinch I was in, was willing to trade me for the bent prop, a thousand dollars, and the extra engine core that came with the plane that Scotty had told me not to part with, (as it was only the first run out, most engines have been rebuilt 10 or 12 times by now). And Chester agreed to ship it right away.

The prop showed up Wednesday morning at about eleven

o'clock. By then, the aircraft mechanic that had not allowed me to fly the bent prop home but was on board to help remove the old prop and install the new one. He also agreed to ship the bent prop back to Chester; for all this help, he charged a hundred dollars, much more than fair. By the time the plane was ready, it was two o'clock, late enough that it wasn't worth leaving since it would start to get dark by five o'clock. Jim, who flew that sexy turbine Ag Cat, suggested that I shoot some landings and he would watch. As I would land and pull up to Jim, he would suggest some improvements on my technique or lack of, then I would do more, and he would make more suggestions. By the time I made half a dozen or more landings, I felt much more in control. I topped off the tank and made ready for the morning.

The sun showed itself with little or no wind and it warmed up nicely that morning. This was the first good day since this whole adventure started. For a minute, it looked like my luck was about to change for the better until I tried to start the plane. The battery was dead! After jumping it and waiting for the engine to warm up, I said my goodbyes, thanking Randy and Jim. They gave me their phone number and pointing over to a twin-engine Cessna, told me if I had any problems, call and they would come to get me. The kindness showed to me by Randy and Jim was unbelievable! It wouldn't be hard to understand how grateful I was.

So with Mom's credit card number in hand, next stop was Huntsville, Alabama, I borrowed the airport's courtesy car, a late 60s or early 70s Cadillac, big as a gunboat and well worn; I chugged my way to the nearest NAPA and bought a battery. From Huntsville, I flew to Monroe, Tennessee. I was able to climb to 7500 feet. on an absolutely beautiful day. The air was smooth, I could see almost forever, the engine just purred, it just felt great, my only regret was I did not have a video camera to record its greatness. Maybe the cold days of scud running with next to no visibility were behind me now.

No big deal, but at Monroe, I borrowed some duct tape from the lady in the office to tape up a fiberglass wingtip, which was cracked and now had ripped open during the flight. It looked like a big goose flapping its wings, and I figured it wouldn't last much longer. This must have upset the lady, so she got two of the hanger rats sitting on a park bench to come over and question me. I assured them that it would be okay. Even NASCAR uses duct tape, and they go over 200 mph. With that, the next stop would be Johnson City- Elizabethton, Tennessee. Once again, the flight was absolutely beautiful. It's impossible to describe the magnificence of the scenery passing by with checkered green and brown fields, winding rivers, spotted towns, and distant mountains, all framed by the two wings of a biplane. If I only had a camera. However, going around the Knoxville airspace on the south side, I elected to go under the airspace's outer ring and above the mountains. On the chart it didn't look like much, but the mountains did seem a lot bigger in reality. It was quite a squeeze, watching the GPS and trying not to cross the circle on the screen and not rub a wingtip on the mountain. I may have crossed over the GPS line just a little, but it was mostly an uneventful trip. When I got over Elizabethton, I couldn't find the runway. Everything looked as it should and the GPS said I was on top of it, but no runway; just a small town. As I got a little lower, I realized that what appeared as the last road in town was the runway, spaced the same distance as the rest of the roads. Rolling out, I noticed dead airplanes lined both sides of the runway; this one missing a wing, that one with no engines the next one, no wheels, then no tail and so on. I parked next to the gas pump. It was getting dark fast, and I wanted to gas up to leave early morning. The office was a small white building; the light was on and the door was open. However, nobody around. I hollered "Anybody home," still nobody. As I walked all over, looking for somebody, anybody, I couldn't help feeling that I had landed in the Twilight Zone! Eventually, I found a guy halfway down the runway edge removing parts off one of the broken-down planes, and he gassed me up.

During the night, while sleeping, bad weather was coming across from the west. I had been watching it on the Weather Channel and knew it would be close. As it was getting light, I was warming up the engine and it started raining. The mountain tops were already in the clouds. The ceilings were only about 200, maybe 300 feet. It was going to be tight, but I thought if I could get going, I should be able to get out in front of the bad weather. For those who don't fly, this was like driving in a thick fog not knowing what may pop up in front of you. Back to the charts, I had plotted a course between the mountains; on paper, it looked ok, but shoo, was it close. With not even a mile visibility, I flew a hundred feet or so over the houses and fields in the valleys, hoping not to hit high wires, or whatever else was out there. I hoped I didn't pick the wrong valley and would be trapped. After sweating it out for about 25 miles, I found route 81. Fantastic! I'll just fly over it and slightly to the right, so I can see the interstate, at whatever altitude I can get, which was not much, a hundred feet or so. One thing for sure, I thought they don't put radio towers in the middle of the road. Somewhere near Bristol, they had a tower, not in the road but only a couple hundred feet to the edge. I just missed the guide wires, and nearly crapped in my pants. Shortly after that, I broke out of the clouds, and unlimited skies prevailed. I had a good ride and landed at a county airport near Roanoke, Virginia. From there to Farmville, then on to Tappahannock. It looked like it would be good flying conditions with the mountains and bad weather behind me the rest would be an easy trip. However, at Tappahannock just like the night before, after I parked by the pumps, I walked to the small white building with the door open, radio playing, and nobody around, I looked around, waited some time, then I punched in St. Mary's County on the GPS. It read 19 miles. I crawled up on the plane and looked in the gas tank, and it looked pretty low, so I waited quite a while, still nobody showed up. So I crawled back up, looked at the fuel again, then crawled in and took off. It's funny how after it is too late, you think things through a little clearer. What if I ran out of gas again? I can't afford to buy another prop; what a dumbass I am. By the grace of God, I had made St. Mary's and parked next to the pump. The lady in the office couldn't get Mom's credit card number to go through. She tried every way, but it wouldn't work. Knowing I was just about home, I gave her cash, and with that, I made it home to Laurel, Delaware. My wife picked me up, and I went straight to work. I made it for the last hour of work on Friday, just two weeks late. I even missed Thanksgiving. When I got home, I emptied my pockets and counted one dollar and seventy-three cents left to spare.

I added this paragraph for all my smart-ass pilot friends who asked me why I didn't bump the starter so that the prop wouldn't be straight up and down, preventing it from getting bent. Let me answer that: Ag-Cat best rate of glide is just a hair better than a falling brick. It was the first time ever flying one, and I just didn't think of it! I guess I am no Chuck Yeager or any other of those great test pilots that could very calmly call on the radio, "Houston, we have a problem" as their ship totally disintegrates all around them, but at least I didn't throw my hands up and scream like a little girl.

Chapter 5
Pulling Up To The Starting Line

Since Bainbridge, we had sold our home of sixteen years and now lived in our travel trailer in a campground near work. November, when it started getting cold, the pipes froze. It was rough getting ready for work, to shower and shave in twenty degrees, I had had enough and told Kay, who was a realtor, to find us a house, apartment, or anyplace livable right away! That same day she found us an upstairs unit of a duplex, whose owner only stayed downstairs in the summer. The place was a real dump in the not-so-good part of town, but it was cheap with heat and electricity included, because the lady just wanted someone in the place to keep the pipes from freezing and keep others out. It was about ten miles away from work, also it was close to the airport where I kept the Ag Cat; in fact, too close, my plane was much louder than the rest, and Kay could hear it from our apartment. The poor Ag Cat was tied down in the freezing rain, wind, and snow at the Laurel Airport, where Ed Young that used rent planes to me and ran the airport, told me I could keep it. But understandably, I could not operate out of the airport since Rob's business was already stationed there, which was fine with me.

Whenever I could scrape up fifty dollars, Ed would sell me twenty-five gallons of gas, and I would go for a ride. Inevitably, Kay would hear me and fuss about the money, so I tried different ways of landing and taking off, but she almost always heard me, even in the winter with the windows closed. One Saturday, I planned to fly up to Joe Jenkins' aircraft junkyard, just a couple miles from my father's home. Dad had made contact with Joe earlier in the week and had permission for me to land. The grass runway was rough, really rough. As I rolled out, I heard a ka-bamm, and the tail dropped way down. That last pothole had broken the tailwheel spring, and I couldn't move the plane. After a couple minutes Dad walked over to see why the plane was not moving with me standing next to it. On our way to find help we took a short cut through the junkyard full of pieces and parts of dead airplanes. About halfway through, an older fellow approached us yelling, "What are you doing in here?" So in trying to establish our legitimacy, I replied, "Are you Mr. Jenkins?" "Don't you Mr. Jenkins me, what are you doing in here?" he said. Thank God, he wasn't holding a gun.

After a little bit of back and forth, with me pointing at the broken airplane, he remembered that Dad had talked to him and that we weren't going to steal airplane parts, he told us it was okay to be at the airport, but nobody is allowed pass the ropes around the junk yard. When Joe had cooled down, he called Al Johnson (the crop duster I had asked for a job and didn't waste any words sending me away) and asked if he had a spare tail spring to loan these "poor fellows." My father and I drove over to Al's and knocked on his door. He opened the door about six inches and pointed down at the tail spring on the step, and then closed the door before I could explain myself. When we returned, we met Dan O'Donnell, a local aircraft mechanic, very friendly and more than willing to help us move the plane off the runway. We lifted the plane's tail and put it on the back of Dan's pickup and he drove it up to the front of the airport. The next week Dan helped us install the new used tail spring that I bought. Once again, my father and I drove to Al's to return the tail spring. We knocked on the door, and again Al opened the door six inches, pointed to the step, said, put it there, and closed the door before I could thank him (I'm thinking he must really hate me).

When we returned to Joe's, Dad sat in the plane, and I talked him through starting it, then he taxied it around a little. I think he really enjoyed that. I was to do a fly-by, and Dad wanted to videotape me. I was going to make a landing, but there was a good bit of wind favoring the shorter crosswind runway that had a pronounced hump or hill in the middle. Still feeling a little nervous in this plane, after all, I still had that unbelievable bounce at Scotty's in the back of my mind, I had gotten lost, not to mention that bent prop on the way home, and the broken tail spring, all in the first fourteen hours of ownership, so I wasn't going to take any chances. Every time I would get ready to touch down, it would be on the upside of the hill, and I knew it would throw me back into the air in such a way that I would return to earth hard, so I would power up and go around and try again. Finally, on the third try, it looked like I was lined up just right to touch down, then when everything was going perfectly, Joe runs out next to the runway waving his arms profusely. At this point in my short career, there is a lot I don't know, but I was pretty sure I knew a wave off when I saw it, so I just flew on back to Laurel. When I got home, I called Dad and asked what happened. He said, "Let me play this for you." Listening to the video, I heard, "Here comes Tim," and a loud roar of my engine, then the background noise of the plane. "Looks like he's going to land on the side runway." Then the engine powering up. "I am not sure why he didn't land, looks like he's going around," more background noise, " here he comes, no it looks like he's not landing" again the engine powering up, more background noise, then "Here he comes" and then in a very loud angry voice from Joe, interrupting Dad, "Put that damn camera down and get him out of here!" Joe had thought I was clowning around buzzing the runway and was upset that I would probably get his neighbors mad at him with all the racket I was making. I called Joe and explained that I wasn't trying to buzz the field and that I was just inexperienced and didn't know how to fly. Joe had been a fighter pilot during WWII. He had even flown P-61 black-widow night fighters, (the widow maker), so I was afraid that he wouldn't understand my fears, but Joe was fine with my explanation. Dad and I always enjoyed stopping in from time to time to visit from then on.

DURING this time, I had been working with the Philadelphia branch of the FAA to get a Part 137 Operator Certificate. One of the requirements is to have a base of operations. I had talked Ramario into letting me use the Delaware banner runway, thinking that I would do my agricultural work in the mornings, and tow banners during the day, since banners normally didn't start until eleven o'clock. Then I could do more crop dusting in the evening if needed. We agreed not to ask the landowner until

I received all the licensing. However, an unnamed operator that served on the pesticide board saw my application for a pesticide license naming Ramario's runway as my base of operations. He had grown up with the landowner, and told him of our plans, and convinced him that I might spill chemicals and ruin the land. Poor Ramario, the landowner really got mad at him for not asking first and almost threw him off the land. I contacted the owner and reassured him that we had no intention of doing this without his permission and the reason we waited to tell him was basically what just happened. Because of the competitive spirit of the other operators, we wanted to keep it secret. He was okay with Ramario but didn't want me operating there. For my plan B, I had worked out a deal with the Georgetown Airport to rent an office at the terminal and a loading spot. I had this in writing, but then a month later, I received a letter denying me the use of the airport, stating that they were trying to attract high tech business and I wasn't a good fit. I can't say for sure, but that same unnamed operator did at times work out of Georgetown, had his base of operations nearby, with deep roots in that area, and may have encouraged the powers to be, to not let me in. The FAA questioned the problems I was having with nailing down my base of operations. When I told them my story, the FAA told me Georgetown couldn't disallow me the airport's use. They said the FAA had given the airport some seven hundred thousand dollars in grants the preceding year. They could demand it back if the airport wasn't there to serve the public. I told the FAA that I didn't want to push the issue, that wouldn't be good press for a start-up business and not the kind of confrontational image I wanted. However, through the construction business, I knew the president of the county council. I stopped in to see him, still feeling slighted. I mentioned that I had in writing both approval and then disapproval letters and that if any other crop duster used that airport after they turned me down in writing, I would sue, "For, I don't know, maybe a couple million." I probably shouldn't have done that, but it did feel good, and for a few years, I would call a friend at the airport to see if any other operators worked out of there.

BY this time, I'd met Gordon Rinner who operated a parachute jump school at Laurel. Gordon was a kindly older fellow who just loved parachuting and being right in the middle of all the hubbub that goes with the party-like atmosphere surrounding the jump zone. Gordon was in the process of moving his business seven miles south to Bennett Airport in Salisbury, Maryland, and he asked me, "Why don't you talk to Bill and Eileen Bennett." The Bennetts were glad to have me, so I told the FAA that I would have to change my base of operations on the application once again. The guys at the FAA, which had been helpful all along, advised me to find a base of operations in Delaware, anywhere in Delaware, so that they could finish the licensing process. Then if I wanted to go to Maryland, they would transfer my Operators Certificate to the Baltimore FAA. But if I wanted to use a Maryland address, they would have put my application and all the other papers in a big yellow envelope and mail it to the Baltimore office, then the process would start all over, I would probably miss the upcoming season.

DAVE, who I had kept in touch with since the day I found him hoeing watermelons, had agreed to let me use his place in Felton, Delaware as a base of operations. I am not sure how well things would have turned out without his help. Meanwhile, in February back at Salisbury, Bill Bennett gracefully moved his planes out of his hanger, and we moved my plane in. Then he hooked me up with David Barrett, a master mechanic that had retired from the Air Force and then retired a second time as chief of maintenance from NASA. You might say he grew up on round engines. To make an application for the Part 137 Agricultural Operations that I needed, the FAA requires that you have at least one airworthy aircraft. This also applies to charter operations, airliners, and flight schools. They will inspect that first plane carefully before issuing an Operators Certificate, but if you buy one or a hundred more planes, they don't inspect them. David and I did a lot of work on the plane, and I had to buy many parts. When he adjusted the compass, he found that it was out fifty-five degrees, which helps to explain why I got so lost on the way home after I bought the plane.

When the FAA came and inspected the plane, David did most of the talking, which was a great help in getting that old plane passed, since they felt comfortable that David had the knowledge to keep the plane safe. They gave us a list of a few minor things to fix before they would pass the plane, like mark the maximum weight on the side of the chemical tank and to placard the compass deviation next to it. Then they told me to send a fax stating that I had made these corrections, then they would complete the application. I was a little perturbed that they wouldn't just pass the plane right then, so I said I could do all these things right now if they just gave me a minute. They smiled and said, you don't understand; we have to create a paper trail to show that the FAA did its job and found some discrepancies, and that you followed through with corrections to put in your file. They said they were sure that I would send the fax before they got back to the office. I hadn't realized what a favor they were doing me.

THE next step was to do a demonstration flight and take a test about agriculture flying. We made arrangements to meet at Dave's airport in Felton, Delaware. That morning I met the two men from the FAA. These guys were from a different department than the inspectors that I had already met, so I was a little nervous. I was trying to make a good impression and using as many twenty-five cent words I could think of, to show that I was a professional. Meanwhile, Dave was telling them that he had added up everything that his ex-wife had taken for divorce, and had divided it by how many times he had gotten sex, he figured it cost him $368.00 each time, and then told some more dirty jokes. While I was sitting at the desk filling out the test, a guy named Barney came in, whom I had heard about. He was real bright, almost a genius, but also a bit of a free spirit and nudist. He asked Dave if he could use the fax machine. Apparently, he had been listening to the Bob and Tom Show in his car and wanted to respond to one of their questions. Bear in mind I am trying to concentrate on the test while Barney is rambling on how many brain cells are lost when masturbating; with all this going on, I thought they are killing my chances of getting a license. After the written test, we went outside, I untied my plane, taxied out, took off, and did a demonstration flight spraying water on the field next to Dave's hanger. Dave had almost two thousand feet of grass runway, up to the hanger where everybody was standing on the gravel driveway that crossed the runway, then the runway continued for another two thousand feet running next to the road. After I finish spraying, I landed a little faster than I should have (it's funny the things you think under pressure). I had it in my mind that if I couldn't land in two thousand feet, they wouldn't think I was much of a pilot, so I was determined to stop before them. I pushed on the brakes as hard as I could without nosing over, but when the plane hit the bump where the gravel driveway crossed, the plane started going off to the left, heading right for a telephone pole. Without a thought, I hit the power, and the engine roared back to life. Then I stomped the rudder with everything I had, then chopped the power. It was unbelievable, it looked like someone had picked the plane up and turned it a quarter turn and put it back down, when all the dust settled I came to rest right over the ropes, exactly to the inch where the plane was when I untied it! I got out of the plane like everything was normal; the FAA guys came over and said they would pass me, "but didn't like the way I was showing off, cowboying the plane around on the ground." A good five years later, I was visiting Dave down in North Carolina. One night at a bar, we met up with another duster that Dave knew. As Dave introduced me to him, Dave said, "This is the guy I was telling you about that almost ground looped on the FAA check ride." I told Dave that I couldn't believe he knew that, he'd never said a word to me about it, and I thought I had totally gotten away with it.

NOW I was an officially licensed crop duster, still hanging out at Dave's. He had a little bit of fertilizer dusting work come in and didn't want to change his plane over since he had spraying to do. Dave asked me if I would change over my plane and do it. This is my first real job and Dave was impressed with how well my 985 light-frame Ag Cat carried full loads. A few days later, Dave gave me my first spray job. It was a nice long narrow field surrounded by tall pine trees, with a housing development on the one narrow end. Dave instructed me that I could spray the long way for ¾ the way down, then pull up and go around the houses, and would just have to spray the last ¼ of the field crossways last, when the plane is lighter to avoid the homes. This made sense to me, so off I went. That first ¾ went great and I was starting to get in a groove, diving straight down over the trees, rounding out just inches over the wheat, heading straight towards the trees, waiting for the last minute to pull up. The plane was performing fantastic and I was having a great time. Next it was time to do the end. I came over the trees and dove down, rounded out perfect, pulled just a little up to get over the irrigation, and pushed back down and leveled out. Just then the engine quit! I looked at the tall trees in front of me and said, "oh shit," then looked at my left hand on the throttle quadrant to be sure the knobs were in the right spot, looked back at the tall trees getting closer, and again said, "oh shit," then I looked at the emergency dump cable and put my hand on it. Once again I looked at the tall trees getting even closer and closer, and again said "oh shit." About then the exhaust made a real loud ka-boom (it sounded like a cannon going off) and the engine started back up, just as I was trying to make a hard left turn. My heart was racing. That was truly a three "oh shit" experience! I figured that the gas was low and had caused the problem, so I flew back to Dave's and topped off my tank and went back to the field and dove in right where I had left off, in exactly the same way, and once again, the engine cut off. After that, I told myself that if I didn't learn how to fly, the engine would probably keep cutting off. Later that day, Dave asked me if I wanted to ride along with him while he met a customer. As we were riding along, I asked Dave if he ever had an engine cut off when he went over irrigation systems. Dave told me that with the gravity-fed airplanes like mine, you couldn't go negative positive negative Gs abruptly or the engine will cut off, then he added you could count to five real slow before it starts back up. Then Dave went on to say I was going to tell you about that, but I thought you knew better!

A couple of days later, a little surge of work came in for Dave, and I was mixing the chemicals and helping him load. His partner Craig came up from North, Carolina with a really sweet 1340 Ag Cat with all the bells and whistles, and was ready to get to work. Now anybody that knew Dave at that time knew he has only two things on his mind: women, and crop dusting, I think in that order! Dave came in for another load. Craig had just parked his plane and had gotten out, and was waiting for Dave's instructions, who was busy gassing up. Just then, Dawn showed up, the woman I had seen hoeing watermelons, and I am assuming did move out. She was beautiful with long blond hair, a very short white dress, and white tights on her long legs. Dave shut off his plane and told Craig and I, "I'll be right back," and Dawn and Dave went into the house next to the hanger. It was close to an hour before they came back out. Meanwhile, Craig was slowly getting uptight; he hadn't been told where or what to spray, so we just stood around. I was stuck in the middle, just listening to Craig spout off. "This is the problem with Dave. He doesn't know where his priorities are." I thought, I know Dave, and I think he just showed us where his priorities were. Craig didn't know it, but a couple of days later, he had gotten even with Dave. Apparently, Dave had bought a new parts washer and had put it in the chemical shed. While Craig was standing around with nothing to do, he filled the parts washer up with avgas. After Craig went back home, early one morning before light, Dave went into the shed to get ready for work, and according to Dave, "The last thing I saw was the little blue spark the light switch made" before the shed blew up!

BACK at Salisbury, I was juggling between working at the pill-plant and trying to get the crop dusting business started, I manage to get a couple of small jobs. For my first job, I sprayed snap beans with Dimethoate, which really stinks, smelling like rotten eggs. Still not having my load center complete, I was keeping the plane next to Bill's office area, with the lounge, bathrooms and coke machines, and I was using a garden hose to fill the plane. That evening Bill came over in his golf cart, while he was talking to me, he got a whiff of that rotten egg smell, and with his deep gruff voice, said, "That stuff stinks." I agreed it did smell a little, and with that he said, "That's it, I'm not putting up with this stink. You'll have to move down to the end of the runway by the trees." So, I have been kicked out already! At first, I didn't know how to take Bill and his direct down to business approach, coupled with that deep gruff voice. I was mostly scared of him, but as I found out, you couldn't ask for a better guy. One night, Bill and Eileen rode down to my end. I had just hooked up my gas tank and pump. Bill told me that any gas at the airport was subject to a ten percent airport tax. It was a good thing Eileen was there; she saw the fire building in my eyes and stopped me before I said something that I would be sorry for, and said, "Don't you know when Bill is joking?"

DAVID Barrett was to meet me at nine o'clock and help me diagnose a miss in my engine; it wasn't a bad miss, so I decided to go ahead and spray a load before he showed up. It was an easy field, open on both ends, with only one lone pine tree next to the river. In a biplane it is hard to know when to pull up as you fly towards the trees, because the top wing blocks your view. So, I judge the height of the trees by how thick they are. Evidently, this tree was very skinny for its height, as I ended up skinning it with my prop all the way up. I also learned that it's probably too late to pull up when you can see the trees over the top wing. After I landed, while I was fixing some broken nozzles, David showed up and couldn't believe all the pine tree branches stuck in my landing gear, and began to lecture me about getting too close to the trees. He really didn't need to; I'd had already made up my mind not to do that again.

ONE of the hurdles that I had to deal with starting my business in this area was Rob my friend and competitor. He was well liked and a little bit of a hot dog in his flying; the farmers were impressed by his abilities and loved to watch him go under the power wires. Because of this, trying to win over some of the farmers, I would try to go under as many wires as I could, especially when people were watching, but the thing is, my plane was five or six feet taller than Rob's. One morning when I went under a wire, there was a mailbox on the other side of the road, and the wires seemed a little lower than usual, not wanting to strike the wire, I held down just a hair too long. I had knocked off a spray boom on the mailbox. When I drove out there to retrieve my boom, luckily nobody was around, but that mailbox was trashed, laying a good three hundred feet out in the field.

The Learning Curve

All I have to say to all you teenagers that have ever been riding around the back roads, drinking, and swinging at mailboxes with baseball bats. Eat your heart out!

Chapter 6
Off And Running

The morning after what I call the perfect day, which I'll tell you about later, I got a call from Colbourn Swift, that had a fair size farming operation in Somerset County. I hadn't heard him right and kept calling him Mr. Smith, he said that he knew I was busy, but did I think I could work his job in. I had very little work, in fact, none that morning, but I didn't want him to think that this wasn't a prospering business, so I told him that I still have a couple of loads left this morning, and then I can meet you. It was killing me to wait a couple of hours before I met him. He was a great guy and never did correct me for calling him Mr. Smith. He gave me eight hundred acres to spray. At that point, I'd been happy with twenty acres, so this was fantastic. Years ago, I was watching a friend of mine who owned a plumbing business talk to a prospective customer. He stated that he was so busy he didn't know if he could fit them in. The more he said he had too much business, the more they wanted him to do the job. Years ago, I told a prospective customer I had a gap in my schedule, and I could start their job right away. The people lost interest, and after that, I always said that I was so busy that I couldn't see straight, and I never lost a job again.

THE next morning, I started in on Colbourn's wheat. The second field was right next to the state prison, as I was going back and forth and turning around next to the guard towers so close that I would wave at the guards. The plane was handling perfectly with full loads in the cool, calm morning. I was just having a great time. When I came back from my third flight and was mixing up the next load, a county police car, and a van with the State of Maryland Agriculture Department emblems on the doors were coming down the long dirt road to my load station. They pulled up to where I was, and a man got out of the police car. He was a little heavyset, wearing mirrored sunglasses, and a full uniform with a shiny oversize badge, and tall black boots. He could have doubled for Jackie Gleason in the movie Smokey and the Bandit, and out of the state van a guy got out. He equally could have doubled for Gleason's son in the same movie. The sheriff looked at me and said, "Boyyyyy!, have you got a license for this stuff." It must have taken a minute and a half to say the word boy. At that time, all that the state agriculture inspector had was a two-inch-thick computer printout in a binder of the licensed pesticide applicators, and he couldn't find my name. I had to stop doing what I was, then take them over to the farmhouse that we just moved into, I rooted through all the unpacked cardboard boxes until I found my license. By the time I finished with them, the wind was blowing too hard to spray, so I had to knock off for the morning. Then I went to Bob's and towed banners for the rest of the day, as I had agreed to work for him that summer, not knowing at the time if I would even get five cents worth of crop dusting business.

The next day after that as I was wrapping up the mornings spray work, once again a car came down that long dirt lane, and pulled up. A man and woman that were well dressed got out. I knew they were there in some kind of professional capacity. As they approached me, they handed me their cards, and they were from the FAA. So here we go again; at least now I knew what cardboard box to find my license in. After looking the plane over, the guy pointed to a hose down on the chemical pump that I had replaced a few days earlier that had NAPA written on it and said, "What's this?" I replied, "That stands for, no aircraft parts available." With a bit of a frown he said, "At least turn it around so we can't see it." I told them that I had, but the other side said Made in Mexico. I just couldn't make up my mind which side was worst. Well, it looks like all the powers to be, know I am in town.

A few days later, I met the Powell Brothers, two older single gentlemen, that farm in Somerset County. They showed me a thirty-five acre field with a telephone pole right smack dab in the middle with the wires going out to all four corners. After scratching my head as to how to get in this spot, I asked them, "Does your combine fit under the wires?" Of course they replied, "Oh yeah." Later I tried to fit the plane under the wires, but the plane was about six inches too tall. The wire hit in the gap between the N strut and the top wing at the same time I had my wheels buried in the sorghum. Instinctively I pulled up. Now the wires were going from the pole up to my left wing, and I was a good hundred feet up, a strange sight, so I braced myself for the take-up when the wire would hit the end. At the same time, while I was looking out the left window at the wire, I heard a crack and caught a glimpse of a blue flash off to the right. While my right hand was steering the plane, I was rubbing my right arm with my left hand, waiting for the take up that thankfully never happened. Then it dawned on me, why was I rubbing my arm? Looking down at my arm, it was peppered with little burns spots from the sparks that looked a lot like welding splatter. It turned out the wires had broken at the right-side pole, and now were dragging through the plane. When the two wire ends touched going through the gap, they sparked and put a big burn spot on the strut. The only other damage was they ripped the wires off the alternator as they passed through. I looked around; only the brothers were watching at the far end, and I didn't think they saw me hit the wires, so I just dove back in and kept spraying, thinking that I got away with it. By now, I had trained Kay to mix the chemicals for the next flight while I flew. When I was spraying the next job, Kay got a call from the power company to see if I was okay. She got really upset, thinking that something had just happened right then, since I hadn't told her about the wires. A couple of years later, when I was using a grass runway in Somerset County, one of my farmers sent his assistant, Wayne, to drop off some chemicals, and Wayne told me that I owed him dinner. When I questioned him about it, he said his wife had been cooking dinner when I hit the wires and the power went out. With dinner only half done, and the power was out for a couple of hours, Wayne had to take the family out for dinner.

I had noticed that it could be dangerous to whistle or hum while I was spraying. Normally this would happen during the last load or two in the evening, after I had been fighting the wind all day, and then the wind would just layout, the flight would turn smooth as silk, and each turn would get tighter and tighter until I was basically hammer-heading each end of the field. Then I would start shooting under all the wires, each pass was getting lower and lower until I felt the wheels hit the crops. The watermelons really made a thump. I was getting more and more aggressive with every pass, feeling great, just full of myself, right in the groove, just pushing all the limits to the max. This would especially happen if people parked to watch, or bystanders were watching. When I finished spraying the field, at a couple hundred feet, I would pass in front of the people and shoot out a paper marker, the markers resemble about 10 feet of toilet paper floating down, then I would whip around and cut it up with the propeller or most of the time I would just catch it with a wing. When I did cut it up with the propeller sometimes I could smell the paper burning on the engine. I would tell myself if I didn't quit whistling or humming, I was probably going to kill myself as I inadvertently got too aggressive. When I would land, Kay would see the paper markers streaming off the plane, and would ask if the kids were out watching again. This slow building aggression reminds me of skiing, playing ball, or racing the go-carts at the beach when I was young. When you get in the groove, it feels so good, and you just can't stop pushing harder and harder until you spin out.

EVERY morning that I didn't have work, I would fly low to Bob's banner strip, drink coffee with his parents, and then fly home low. The next day I would fly low to the Crisfield airport or to my friend Tom Miller's runway. Later in the day, I would ride around doing sales work under that same flight path, so that the farmers thought I had plenty of work. I really enjoyed Bob's parents, they had good stories, and I think they had done or seen just about everything. His father reminded me of the energizer bunny on the TV commercial; a smaller guy who never quit, always had something going on from sunup to sundown. His eyesight wasn't all that it used to be, but that didn't slow him down. He would run over things with the mowers and tractors or run into things, and Bob would have to stop whatever he was doing to fix what the problem was. I loved hearing Bob and his father go back and forth, which happened often: "Ah look, I found my wrench in your shop."

"No it's not, I bought it last year."

"No, that was the blue one."

"No, remember you left that one under the combine."

"No, that was the brown one" and on and on.

Bob's mom would say just about anything. On the fourth of July, some of the pilots had a campfire and were shooting fireworks, so she told the pilots about the time Poppy was shooting off fireworks, and one landed in her lap. She told the pilots that she thought there would be a bush fire. I wish you could see the shocked look on the pilot's faces!

Bob and I both had been self-employed most of our working lives and normally the one in charge. We are used to doing things our own way. Because of that, we were always bickering over the way things got done. I wanted to start on the top and he wanted to start at the bottom, or I turn left first then right, but he wants to turn right first then left. I always figured that it was just a question of technique and not personal. Sometimes I think Bob would take my criticism too personally. Still, I always respected Bob for his values as he always put his family first before business or anything else. Even though one time he left me early in Nashville, tossing me the rental car keys, "See you later." He had had his test a day before I took mine and wanted to get back to his family ASAP.

Tom Miller and his wife Chris were always glad to see me, and I always loved stopping by for a cup of coffee. Tom had a lot of stories, and I know they were true. I think there is nothing that Tom hadn't tried, such as the aerobatics he used to perform in his ultralights. I have seen the bent, twisted remains of those aircraft that he somehow walked or crawled away from. He used to do a lot of parachute jumps, if not jumping he would fly the jumpers up. On occasions he and a guy named Scholz used to fly jumpers up in a DC-3 and had done barrel rolls in that plane. They had also ran out of gas and landed in the Route 13 median strip in that DC-3, then walked to the nearest gas station to get gas.

I used to keep all of the empty boxes that the chemicals came in, then stack them neatly up like it was new work at my mixing station. I would see my competitors flying by, checking out how much work I had. When I would see them at meetings or different places, they would say things to me in such a way that I knew they were upset by how much work they thought I had. If they only knew the boxes were empty.

ONE evening after I finished my last job, I stopped by Tom Miller's, and as always, he offered me a glass of iced tea. We sat and talked a little while, then I fired the plane back up and headed home. It had been a great day, I had gotten a lot of work done, the weather was good with low winds, and I was doing everything that I had dreamed of. When I got home, feeling all fat, dumb and happy, Kay started giving me holy hell, just about ripping my ears off, as I climbed out of the plane. Apparently, she had been timing me, knowing that I only carried just barely over one hour of gas, and I had been gone for almost two hours. Kay had called the farmers in the area and had them riding around looking for me in their fields and trees. After that, every time I stopped by Tom's, he would call Kay and tell her that I was there, before he would talk to me.

GAS was always an issue; before I did anything getting ready to fly, I always gassed up first as a habit. One day after spraying a field about twenty miles away and returning to load up to do the second half, a farmer was waiting for me when I landed. Instead of gassing up, like I always did, I climbed down to talk to the farmer, and when we finished talking, I pumped the chemicals in and took off. I sprayed the other half of the field and head-ed for home. That was the last job of the morning, so I leaned back in the seat, just relaxing, watching all the scenery go by as I crossed the river. I happened to glance at the fuel gauge, and it was dead on empty. All of a sudden, I wasn't relaxed anymore. The corn was getting tall, and I didn't want to risk flipping the plane if I landed in it, so I tried to fly next to the bean fields if I had to land. It's better to go next to a field rather than directly over the field. If the engine quits, you can normally get into the field a little to either side, but if you are right over a field, you may not be able to turn around in time to get back to the field. I headed right for Rob's place; it was the closest and I made it. I gave him the only ten bucks I had on me and put in five gallons of gas. I took off downwind because it was pointing towards home, at about half throttle to save gas. When I got home and gassed up, it took thirty-two and a half gallons, and the tank holds thirty-three. This means I would have come up short four-and-a-half gallons had I tried to go straight home instead of to Rob's.

Another time I had to spray twenty-five acres in four different places, down by Wallops Island, a little farther away than usual. I had sprayed fifty-acre and sixty-acre fields before in that area, and fuel was tight but manageable, so I didn't think much of it. When I was on the last field, I notice that fuel was getting low, so I told myself one more pass and I am getting the hell out of here, but then I was only a pass away from being done, so I did another pass. Then there was only one small place left to spray and the job would be done perfectly. So, I turned around and headed back in for another pass. All done, I headed for home. Halfway home, I passed over an airstrip that I didn't know the owner, thinking should I land there, once again looking at the fuel gauge. "Ah, it will be ok," and I kept going. Then halfway between that airstrip and home where neither is closer, it seemed like the needle just jumped to E. The last couple miles I would being flying over a section that passes many housing developments, so I started a slow, easy climb and got up to two thousand feet, just in case the engine quit. Luckily, I made it home, and the engine quit just as I pulled on the pad. Most anybody in this business will tell you that it is easier and quicker to spray a hundred-acre field than a ten-acre field, with all the extra time spent turning around, and this really brought the point across.

FLYING the parachute jumpers for Gordon wasn't much different. One day I was helping out during a really busy spell. The guy that flew the jumpers full-time handed off the plane that he had been flying. While he got another plane ready, he told me it had enough gas to carry the jumpers three more times. Whether I took too long or went too high, I don't know, but on the way down after the second bunch jumped out, the plane ran out of gas and quit. After I landed, Gordon met me in his car, and with a piece of rope, we towed the plane back down the runway and up to the gas pump. As Gordon gassed up the plane, he lectured me that it takes seven gallons of gas for each trip up, while he pumped fifteen gallons in, and told me I had enough for two trips. I thanked him for the whole extra gallon, but when he wasn't looking, I put more gas in.

COMING home one mid-summer evening, I passed over a field that Rob in his Pawnee was just finishing. Within minutes Rob pulled up beside me, waved, then pulled away. I threw the throttle forward. I wasn't going to let him beat me, but he left me behind. The next time I saw him, I said that I was disappointed that when I applied full power, the plane didn't seem to go any faster. He said he thought he saw the nose drop a little. A few weeks later I was given seventy acres to spray of a hundred and forty acre field. In the middle was an irrigation pivot that two brothers shared, but each brother only tended their seventy acre side. I had no sooner than made my first pass for the brother on the left side, when along comes Rob in his Pawnee spraying the right side for the other brother, so I timed it so I would jump back in for my next pass when Rob started his. The little impromptu race was a blast. Rob's plane was faster and would pull away from me on the straight away, but I could turn around on a dime. I ended up doing four passes to his three. Boy, how I love that old light-frame Cat.

ALL that horsing around was hard on the plane. One season of hard ag flying is probably the equivalent of ten years wear and tear on a normal plane. One day I notice that the rpms would go up a little when I dove in the field, and the rpms would go down a little when I pulled up; with a constant speed prop, the rpm should never change, so when I landed, I greased the prop. The older counterweight props could stick and react slowly if you didn't grease it enough. The saying is "grease, grease, and grease some more," and when it quits throwing grease on the windshield, grease it some more. But this rpm fluctuation continued. It wasn't much, but I could tell something wasn't just quite right, and when the plane was idling, the stick had a different vibration. This went on all day, and I kept checking things and greasing the prop. I even clamped on the paddles and had Kay help me work the prop with the paddles, where one pushes and the other pulls together, then reversing, changing the prop pitch back and forth. This requires some coordination; maybe you married men can imagine how difficult it is not to yell at the wife who couldn't seem to get coordinated with me. But I couldn't put a finger on the problem. That evening I was taking off on the back runway. As I passed over a small bump, the whole engine flipped up in front of me! Then it slammed back down, and then flipped up again, then slammed back down before I could chop the power. Luckily, I had enough runway left to stop. It turned out, both bottom bolts holding the engine mount to the plane had broken, and with full power on take-off, the engine had pulled away from the plane hinging on the top mounts, making the engine flip up. As the engine went up, it stretched the throttle linkage attached to the firewall, cutting the power and causing the engine to slam down. Once down, the throttle linkage would power up the engine to start the process over. I suspect that only one bolt was broken all day, allowing the engine to move just a little, pulling on the linkage making the rpm change slightly. I replaced the bolts by using Kay's car jack and a piece of 4x4 to jack the engine up, to make room to slide the new bolts in place. However this problem would persist for the next year, at least half a dozen times, causing me to make some emergency landings. One morning when I dove in extra hard over a tall tree and rounded out, with a really hard bamm, another bolt broke, I flew home careful not to make any abrupt maneuvers and fixed it. After that, I tried not to round out so hard, and the bolts didn't break as often. I think gyroscopic procession had a lot to do with it, just as it gets some people when the tail comes down on landing, causing some to ground loop. The gyroscopic procession is the propeller acting like a big gyroscope resisting change of direction, more noticeable with larger props. I'd had learned to feel that different vibration and catch the broken bolt before I take off. The next year I had the engine mount remade one inch bigger, eliminating the one-inch spacer, and used grade nine bolts from a Caterpillar bulldozer. Since that I never had that problem again.

I wonder if manhandling the plane so hard had caused other problems, such as the one evening when I had to spray a field surrounded by tall pine trees. Because the wind had completely laid out, I dove in the middle of the field and put out a puff of smoke to determine which way the wind drifted so I could start on the field's upwind side, and not get the spray all over the windshield. I pulled up, went around to the upwind edge, proceeded to dive in and spray, but when I pushed the stick forward, it just went ka-thump, and nothing happened; I pulled back and ka-thump, nothing; I moved it a couple more times in disbelieve: ka-thump, ka-thump, ka-thump, ka-thump. My first thought was, thank God it didn't happen thirty seconds ago, or I would be plastered against the pine trees. Then my thoughts went back to what do I do now! When you have a big problem in training, they teach you to dump the load, so I thought about that and decided that the plane was stable now and would stay more stable with the weight so I didn't dump the load.

A few months earlier, when I was doing a biannual review and was just about done, the instructor said that we had to kill ten more minutes, "so go ahead and do whatever you want." I said, let's land as if we lost the elevator control and only use trim and power to land. The approach was good, but as I tried to flare out, I got caught up in these up and down oscillations, chasing them with the power. I suppose had it been an emergency, we could have landed, but it wouldn't have been pretty. This was in the back of my mind, thinking that really that didn't work out well. Then I thought maybe I should land at Salisbury with the longer runway, but Tom Miller's runway was only half a mile away, and grass. I have always been more comfortable on grass runways. As I came across the field leading up to Tom's runway, there was a ditch at the beginning of the runway, and it looked like my wheels might hit it. I gave the engine just a couple of hundred rpms and then took it back out, fearing that I might start those up and down oscillations, but it arrested the descent just enough to clear the ditch. Then I touched down smooth as silk. It was one of the best landings ever.

Tom came out to meet me and offered me a glass of iced tea. I said I had a problem with the controls and he watched me moved the stick foreword ka-thump and back ka-thump a couple of times. Tom asked, "so?" then I told him to watch the elevator and I moved the stick again, but the elevator didn't move. Tom looked at me with amazement and then said I'll call Kay. Only two bolts attach the elevator bellcrank, and one was missing. With the bolts being just one inch from the pivot point, when one is gone, the elevator rotates on the remaining bolt instead of moving. Tom found me a bolt and gave me another glass of iced tea, and I went home. There is an A.D. (airworthiness directive, FAA service bulletin) to replace these bolts every sixty hours of flight, and this had been done. I believe removing the bolts so often has worn the holes they go in, so I did the modification and welded a new three-bolt bell crank on and never had that problem again.

THE evening before the fourth of July, as I was taking off, passing the end of the runway, just beyond the point of no return, the engine went Ka-bamm and then Woppa Woppa Woppa and next blue smoke went everywhere. I looked down, and saw I was over the old rubble pit. "Thank you Lord!" I pulled the emergency dump, turned the plane around, by now the windshield was covered with oil and I couldn't see a thing. Luckily, I am just a little claustrophobic, and I had removed the left window; I stuck my head out the window so I could see to land and got a head full of hot oil, but I was able to see enough to land. As I parked at the loading pad, Kay came out and wanted to know why I was back so soon. "I know you didn't finish that job yet." Thinking your all heart, I pointed to all the smoke. She just looked and said, "so what?" I guess she didn't care if I flew with a blown engine, but I've got my limits. The top of a cylinder had blown completely off, and that seemed to be a sign of what was yet to come.

A couple of days later, after I had replaced the blown cylinder, I called Howard the farmer we were working for, and asked if I could charge more chemicals to his account. I said that I would deduct it from my flying bill, explaining that it was my fault that the chemicals were dumped over the old rubble pit, and I would pay for it. Howard insisted he would pay for the chemicals, and after some debate, he let me pay for half. I don't know how many other guys would treat me that well. Howard was one of a kind, he always said what he thought and could be a little rough in how he got things done, but somewhere along the way, he crossed the line from customer to friend. The first time I met him, he told me he would give me work, but he wouldn't pay me right away. I said, "You are going to pay me some time, aren't you?" He said yes. So, I replied, "Good enough for me." I might add that he always paid me just like clockwork.

THE evening before Labor Day weekend, I was spraying a field next to Route 50. Cars were bumper to bumper in route to the beach, not moving at all; this was normal on Friday evening. Half a dozen of the cars had pulled over, and the people had gotten out to watch me spray. I could see the flash of their cameras going off as I went by. But something wasn't right. The plane had a strange vibration and the engine was undered powered. It was hot, the air was thin, the plane was heavy, my turn arounds took forever, and I could feel the plane just wanting to fall right out of the sky. At one point, I flew the half-mile to the airport to land and to figure out what was wrong with the plane, but then thought if something was wrong, I wouldn't be able to finish the job, so I returned to finish spraying. I just remembered thinking about the people watching me with amazement, if only they knew how sloppy I was flying this evening. After I landed, I figured that I had a stuck valve. The banner planes have this problem on a regular basis due to the salt air. I stood in front of the engine, wet my finger, and began to touch each rocker cover, feeling for a cold cylinder, touching one, pssss--- nope, touching another, pssss--- nope, another, pssss--- nope, another, pssss--- nope, and another, holy crap! I can stick my whole hand right through the cylinder. That's right, another blown cylinder! My thought was, if from now on I didn't work the night before a holiday, maybe I wouldn't blow so many cylinders. The next morning, I got up extra early, took the broken cylinder off, and started installing the new one. Then I had to go to Ocean City and pull banners all day. I returned around dinner time and finished installing the cylinder and hooking up everything associated with it. And still had time to spray two fields before dark.

TOWARDS the end of the summer, I started getting enough business that it was tough to pull the banners and still get all the spraying done. However, I wanted to live up to my agreement with Bob to work the whole summer pulling banners, so often I would fly my plane to Bob's instead of driving, even though the gas my plane burned cost more than what I would make that day pulling banners. One morning the last spray job was a little past Bob's, almost at the beach. After finishing the spray work, I could just land at Bob's and report to work. Passing over

Bob's I noticed the windsock had the wind pretty strong out of the southwest, and that lined up with Bob's taxiway. While I was spraying, the wind died out, and the job had gotten a little more enjoyable. I was turning around over the bay, enjoying the scenery, and just generally feeling good. When I returned to land at Bob's, I looked down and saw several of the banner pilots standing around, and still in that euphoric moment I decided to show off. I whipped around and landed right over the pilots on the short four hundred foot taxiway, into the wind, but the wind had fallen out. Due to the lack of wind, I had landed a little fast, but I didn't worry, thinking that I could turn about 30 degrees slightly to the left onto the runway. However, I'd had just installed a new locking tailwheel, due to Bill Bennett fussing about all the holes that my tail wheel made in his runway as the tail wheel shimmied like a shopping cart wheel. Every time I landed, Bill said it looked like a golfer taking a big slice of grass with the swing. The way the new lock worked, the tailwheel was locked, so it would only go straight ahead until the stick was pushed all the way forward, then it would release, free to swivel. Because I was on the brakes hard, it was necessary to pull back on the stick to keep from flipping the plane up on the nose. That new lock wouldn't allow the plane to turn onto the runway, so the plane went straight into a ditch headfirst and stopped with the tail sticking straight up in the air.

The worst thing is, I had to listen to Bob and Karl lecture me on my decision-making abilities. After a while, Bob got a rope, and just like Roy Rogers, he lassoed the tailwheel, hooked the rope to his Kubota tractor, and pulled the plane back down and then out. Bob and I discussed what to do next, and he kept insisting that I have a mechanic look it over before I flew it again. I insisted that everything looked just fine. As we were going back and forth, Bob's nephew, Ralph pointed to the right cabane strut and asked if it was supposed to be buckled? Maybe Bob had a point, so I had a new piece sent next-day air. Hun, a waterman turned plane mechanic, volunteered to help me install the strut. The top wing and gas tank center section had shifted forward, and we had to pull it back to get all the bolt holes lined up. Looking around, we found a piece of banner rope and tied it to the center section and to the frame near the tail, stuck a piece of 2x4 in the middle, and twisted the rope until it pulled everything back in place; it worked great. Bob was totally beside himself, because he felt that only a proper aircraft mechanic should do the repair. Twisting an old piece of rope, out in a cornfield with a waterman directing just didn't seem the same as the typical aircraft maintenance shop with the white epoxy floors and rolling tool chests full of all kinds of specialty tools and highly trained men in uniforms doing the repair, but I was on a tight budget.

BACK in the middle of the summer I had gotten another call from Colbourn Swift asking me if I knew anything about cover crop seeding. Of course, I said "Oh yeah, I have done that lots of times." I thought I had plenty of time to buy a spreader and figure it out before it was time to start. In the preceding year, there had been a fish kill caused by pfiesteria bacteria, and the state had started a cover crop program paying the farmers to plant cover crops in the two lower counties. Broadcasting the seeds by air through the standing crops made sense because if they waited for the farmer to harvest the existing crop and then plant the cover crop that helped prevent field erosion into the waterways, sometimes it could be too late. The first frost would cause the cover crop to go dormant before it grew enough to do any good. By air the seeds could be dropped sooner through the standing crop, and often the cover crop would be well developed several inches tall when they harvest the existing crop. I copied the state applications and went door-to-door asking the farmers if they signed up for this gravy money, and I ended up with more cover crop work than I knew what to do with. I flew cover crop seeds from sunup to sundown for a month and a half, literally starting the engine as it was getting light and shutting it off as it got dark.

WHEN I had started this venture, I had met Libby Hastings a friend of the Bennetts whose husband had recently passed away, and he had had several nice aircraft that she sold. Now she had empty space and thought she could use the extra money. Libby lived in a large house on the only hill around, about a half-mile from our farmhouse, with really nice grass runways and hangers. She had asked me if I would be interested in renting her hangers and runway. I took a look at the white epoxy floors and teak wood walls on the hangers and grass on the runway that look manicured, and I knew this was not a good fit for a crop dusting operation. I would run into her occasionally, and one time she said that she heard me go over every morning. For the longest time, every morning I would warm the plane up for fifteen or twenty minutes, do a mag check, and when everything was fine, take off. But just as I was passed the end of the runway, the engine would cough several times and eventually straighten up. Not knowing if the engine would quit, I would pass over Libby's runway on my way just in case, but I didn't tell her why. Once I started covering the engine with a tarp every night, the problem went away; the dew was getting in the mags and not making a problem until vaporizing after they heated up.

WHEN I bought the light-frame Ag Cat I didn't understand the difference in the various models, I just knew I wanted an Ag Cat. I had picked the light-frame mostly because the price was right. After flying other models, I fell in love with that light-frame that had the short engine mount. In this part of the country with small irregular shapes surrounded by tall objects, it is the perfect fit for this area. It was extremely agile and could get out of tight spots, much like driving an MG or small British sports car instead of a Mack truck. When the chemical tank reached less than half full, it really just turned into a little rocket ship. I would pull up hard at the end of the field, go not more than two hundred feet up, then kick the left rudder hard, push the stick over hard and come back down just fifty feet away from the last pass, and spray going the other way. One day when the tank ran below the halfway point, I was doing just that when the stick lock swung down and blocked the stick from going over. By the time I shoved the stick lock up out of the way and was able to push the stick over, the plane had run out of speed and was getting ready to come down ass first. I am sure if I had been in any other plane than that light Cat, I would not be here to write this, and that is not the only time that plane forgave me.

THE Brinsfield's were some of my first customers and lived about two miles across the Nanticoke River. Their large farm complex was split in half by the dirt lane. Balvin, that was my age and his parents farmed together on the right as you entered. On the left was Balvin's cousins, John and Howard, two brothers farming together, and across the road was Russell, their uncle. All of them were just a joy to be around, particularly Balvin Sr. and his wife. They always invited me in for a drink or something to eat. Mrs. Balvin Sr. was a pistol. She always spoke her mind and to the point. The one thing I could never figure out was that I could mail them a bill in the afternoon from my town and get the check tomorrow in the mail from their town. It is just impossible, and I used to check the postmark, thinking that the only way I could get the check that fast is if she drove it to my mailbox, but the postmark would be on it. I still scratch my head on that one.

One day John rode me around in his pickup and showed me about twenty acres of pepper sprouts in the middle of a field that he wanted me to spray with the rest of the field not ready to be sprayed yet. When I showed up to spray, I just couldn't make out which ones. The sprouts were too small to see from the plane; even diving in and looking, I just couldn't make heads or tails out of it. After circling and looking, I had enough and landed on the dirt road, which turned out to be more sand than dirt. I climbed out, went around to my right wing, pulled some paper markers out of the flagger, walked over to the peppers, and started marking where they started and ended. When I looked across the field towards the plane, I could see a dust cloud trail going towards the plane, so I went back to the plane to see what the commotion was. There was John in his pickup looking for me, upset, thinking I had crashed. Whenever I would spray his fields after that day, John would stake the area to be sprayed using computer paper to create corners and big arrows. He must have used half a box of computer paper each time! From the air, it looked like a football field. I flew over that dirt road with the tall trees on each end one day much later and couldn't believe that I landed there with a half load; I don't think I would nowadays.

On another morning Russell called to see if I had sprayed his snap beans yet, even though I had just gotten the job the night before. Russell was very proactive and always called before I could get the work done. I looked out the window at the big tree by the house, and it was just about bent in half from the wind blowing, so I told him it's too windy, but you will be first when the wind quits. Russell replied, "It's not windy at my house." Boy, if I had a dollar for every time I heard that! I told my wife, Kay, I don't care if there is a hurricane over there; I am going to spray it, so off I went in a huff. When I got over to Russell's only ten miles away, there wasn't even a leaf moving, and it was dead calm.

Another time I was telling Balvin that the power transmission lines going through his farm, and just about all his other farms, almost got me when I went under them, only to find a rusty irrigation end gun on the other side. I told him that the rusty color was hard to see, and suggested they paint it red.

He told me about Denny a crop duster that used to do his work until Denny retired. He said he had been watching Denny years ago go under the wires several times one hot summer day, but as the day got hotter, the lines expanded and sag lower and lower. Finally, about two o'clock, he saw Denny try to pass under again, but this time he saw a big puff of dust. Denny had wrecked his plane, where the wires had gotten too low for the plane to fit. Being concerned, he rushed over and asked Denny what he could do to help. Denny replied, you can take me back to my shop so that I can get my other plane out; I have a lot of work to get done!

Sid, Denny's father had a successful crop dusting business many years ago. When Sid died in a airplane crash Denny took over the business. Because they were well-liked and I have the same kind of plane as they had, and now I serviced the same area that they had, I had benefited from Sid and Denny's great reputation, even though the farmers thought they both were crazy. The farmers told me their planes always did a better job than "Those new single-wing planes."

THAT first year I had fun, like when I would pass over my brother-in-law's house and just fill the tree in the front yard with paper markers. For some reason, the paper in the trees really bugged him, and he would spend a lot of time and effort getting every last one out of the tree. Or the time I made a sneak attack on farmer Mike in his combine, coming in from behind on the right side at eye level and rolling left, almost rubbing the wingtip on his windshield. Mike told me never to do that again, that he thought with all the noise he heard before he saw me that the combine was blowing up. I had gotten pretty good with the markers; I could put them in the back of a moving pick up, or across the windshield, or in my friend's Steve's swimming pool. All though I did waste sixty cents that each marker cost, every time I shot one out. It was always fun to buzz my favorite farmers in the middle of a field on their tractors. It actually got to the point where the farmers were upset with me if I didn't buzz them. I enjoyed laying down a smoke trail as I passed a farmer on a tractor upwind and then pull up and watch the tractor emerge out of the smoke. One farmer laughing told me that when I smoked his son, who was driving the tractor, the son thought I sprayed him, went home, and took a shower.

Speaking of showers, I must tell one on Rob, who was spraying beans one day in his Pawnee, and got too low and hung his wheels up in the beans, causing him to flip the plane over, upside down, and get some nasty chemicals all over him. He ran to the nearest house, knocked on the door, and when a lady answered, not even knowing him, he just ran past her into the house, yelling "emergency" and jumped in the lady's shower. What I would have given to see the look on that lady's face.

THE same year I started, Salisbury Airport put in a control tower and established a six-mile ring around it to be controlled. I had to call and get permission on the radio first for every field I sprayed inside the area. The guys in the control tower were great, and they were always accommodating, helpful, and easy to talk to, which was good because I was lousy on the radio, not knowing all the right lingo. They just wanted to help and make everything run smoothly and safely. All too often, at other control towers the guys let that word "control" go to their heads and think they own the airspace and want you to beg to use it. For that reason, I enjoyed working with the guys in the Salisbury tower. Normally if I needed to pass through their area, I would call them, and they would say, "You are approved to transition through the Class D airspace. Report passing the airport." One evening I called in to pass through in route to Snow Hill to spray a field. After giving me the usual clearance, he added that he had a new guy in the tower that didn't know what an Ag Cat looked like and asked if I could come closer to the tower on the way back so he could see the plane. On the way back, I passed the tower with my wing just inches off the tower glass windows, and very calmly called on the radio, "Six o one Yankee passing the airport." Then I heard some tee-heeing over the radio, and then he cleared his throat. "Roger six o one Yankee. We got you in sight!"

Chapter 7

Dragging Rags

After checking the oil, gassing up, and four new hooks, I took off in the banner plane, swung around, picked up a banner, and headed for the beach. As I started the run along the beach in the typical banner plane with no side windows, doors, or engine cowling, I could see the yellow handle of the oil dipstick slowly turning with the engine vibrations. Eventually, the thing totally unscrewed itself, then started bouncing up and down; as it did, oil started covering the windshield until it was hard to see; I became concerned that the plane would run out of oil and quit. Once I reached Fenwick Island at the end of the route, I climbed up to cruising altitude, turned over the bay, and headed back to the farm. I trimmed the plane a little nose up, grabbed hold of the cross brace with my left hand in the ceiling and climbed out of the doorway on the right with my left foot now on the outside step, and reached around to the engine with my right hand to screw the dipstick back in. While I was screwing the thing back in, the plane made more or less a wing-over to the left and headed for the bay. The centripetal force caused my foot to come off the step. Now I was hanging on only by one hand with the plane pointing straight at the water. I had to pull myself in enough to regain control. It took all my strength, and I almost didn't make it. When I got back to the farm and checked the oil, it wasn't even a quart short. Turns out that just a small amount of oil on a windshield can really look like a massive amount from the inside.

FLYING on a daily basis other than picking up or dropping banners, it can get boring moving at such a slow pace. To pass the time, I would see how slow I could go, with the banner's drag, but the engine still turning pretty good, and keeping some air moving over the wings. It is possible to go so slow at such a high angle of attack that air quits going in the pitot tube; the airspeed gauge would read zero, and if there were any headwind, the people on the Boardwalk would be moving faster than me. On a calm day, I could steer the plane from one end of the beach to the far end by holding my hand out either window and never touch the controls. I would check out the women on the beach, but the thing is you are close enough to see there are scantily clad women down there, but not close enough to really get a good look! To solve this terrible pressing problem, I got hold of a pair of binoculars one day, but with the plane's vibrations, it is tough to focus on anything; everything is just bouncing around. Then more upsetting, I found out that all the women I could see and had tried to see for these weeks, when through the binoculars were the size of beached whales! The moral of this story is sometimes it's better to let your imagination do the work.

SOMETIMES two planes would pull their banners in tandem,

where we would try and line the first and second banner so that from the beach the writing appeared as one sentence. I liked being the second plane; it is difficult to get the plane at the exact speed as the lead plane. While looking through your prop while following another plane, if you can get your prop turning the same rpms as the lead plane, his prop will appear to quit turning, or if yours is slightly faster or slower, his will appear to turn forward or backward (like the wagon wheels in the movies that appears to turn backward). I wonder if you could calibrate a tach this way? The lead edge of the banners have a pole attached from top to bottom, this keeps the banner stretched out, to make sure it was easy to read. These lead poles normally stuck out above and below the banner about a foot. In the second plane I would see how many times I could lightly touch the lead pole from the first banner with one of the 4" round inspection covers on the underside of my wing, or I would climb up the rope a little and push it down with my wing to get the other pilots attention.

I have learned many different things with each new job. For instances you fuel up the plane and put four hooks on it, and now you can tow banners for two and half hours before it's time to land. The thing is, fifteen minutes after taking off I had to pee, not just an ordinary pee, but a pee that demanded all my attention; I think the pee had backed up in my bladder and now was backing up to my brain, consuming every thought. It didn't matter whether I was in a plane towing a banner, in a spaceship, submarine, or the Titanic headed for an iceberg, I had to pee first before steering the ship. So I tried to fold the door down of the Super Cub and maneuver myself rolling partway out the side of the plane and pee, but the air currents carried the pee back all over me. Desperately, I tried to develop a plan B. Looking at the floorboard, I could see light coming up from several holes, so having no other choice I peed in the floor, hoping it would run out the holes. Even this was no easy job since the good Lord didn't oversize my equipment, causing me to try to somewhat stand up in the seat, but not too much so I wouldn't push the stick forward, but enough so I could miss the edge of the seat. After I landed, I filled an old Coke bottle with soapy water, dumped it on the floorboard, found an old empty antifreeze jug, and tied it to a string behind the plane's seat like the rest of the pilots. Problem solved! Sometime after the season was over towards winter, I was helping the maintenance mechanic Robby do his annual inspections; as he was crawling around under that plane, he yelled out, "Tim, this plane stinks like piss, have you been peeing in it." I couldn't believe that a half-year later and after rinsing it with soapy water, it still smelled. Not being able to think of a good answer, I just responded, "Well yes, but only once."

It is also good to pay attention to which plane you're in, as it wasn't uncommon to switch planes. One day I took the little Cub while the one I normally flew had maintenance. The plane I was used to just had an on-off gas valve, which normally I didn't touch, where the little Cub had left or right tanks, making it necessary to switch tanks halfway through the flight. After dropping the second banner of the day and hooking the third, I rounded out at a couple of hundred feet. As the banner took up, the engine coughed and went silent. Luckily my left hand just automatically went up and turned the valve without even a thought, the engine came back to life, and the plane went on without any trouble.

OCCASIONALLY, we got something different, like when some guy wanted a banner towed at a certain time and place at the beach. "Will you marry me?" Somehow the bride-to-be found out and hired another banner towed just a minute or later. "Hell No, I Will Not Marry You." I hope she was kidding!

ONE weekend Bob asked me to pull banners up at the Dover NASCAR races. He had agreed to subcontract for some New Jersey banner company, so I flew there to a private strip only a couple of miles away from the races and picked up a banner. When I got to the stadium with the first banner, there were already three planes circling with banners, plus an ESPN helicopter going back and forth filming the race. There was also the state police chopper circling a couple of hundred feet over the crowds. I fell in behind the other banner planes circling about seven hundred feet, which I believed to be okay since Bob had his waver posted on the office wall that states we must be a least five hundred feet. The state police told us over the radio the ESPN chopper was fussing that the banner planes were getting in his way.

After a while, I went back to the grass strip, dropped the banner, swung around, and picked another up. While I was doing this, the state police chopper had landed, and they were talking to the ground guy who sets up the banners. After I picked up the second banner, it wouldn't pull right as it was laying flat. I didn't know if he had left the weight off the bottom of the lead pole, so I had to drop it and land. By this time, the police had boarded the chopper and were getting ready to leave and saw me land. They got back out and came over to me. "We just wanted to tell you to fly higher. We've already told the other guys over at the other airport." They had gotten back out to tell me because the field hand was Mexican and didn't speak good English, and they weren't sure he understood. I had given them the "Yes sir and no sir" and "I sure will." They were satisfied and preparing to leave when Rick, the banner owner from New, Jersey landed, got out, and started fussing with the police, stating that they were not allowed to stop us in the middle of operations, part 91 section such and such, just giving the police a rash of shit. This totally undid any goodwill I had achieved, then they looked over towards the planes and back at us. "Are those things even legal." This is understandable; if you have ever seen a banner plane up close, there are no doors, no windows, no metal covering around the engine area, many patches all over the plane with different colors, and pretty dirty. "Let me see your license and registration" came next.

As dumb luck would have it, that morning when I came to work, Bob proudly said, "Look what I got you." Then he and the other pilots walked over to the plane and showed me the new seat cover he had installed, which looked nice. As I got ready to go, I picked up the old seat cover lying in a heap on the floor, thinking "you pigs" under my breath, and carried it to the dumpster. I never stopped to think that all the paperwork and registrations were in the back pocket of that old cover!

Yes, I came up short on the license and registration as apparently, Rick didn't have his either. I tried to explain the seat cover deal but got nowhere. I called Bob and let the police talk to him. After a little going back and forth, they agreed it would be okay if Bob faxed the papers to their office. I was told to stay put until they received the papers, and then they would let me know, and I could fly. As soon as they left, Rick took off about

3 minutes later and picked up a banner and went back to the races, I waited about forty-five minutes, still no word, so took off and flew the around about way back to Bob's, so as not to go anywhere near the racetrack. Returning to Bennett's that afternoon, I told the King Air pilot what happened, and he told me to tear the NASA paper out of the back of my FAR/AIM book, fill it out, and mail it certified first thing Monday morning. If a pilot reports any discrepancy or deviation from the rules on this form first, the FAA will not violate you. I called Bob and asked what he thought. He said don't stir the pot, and that he knew the FAA guys and would talk to them for me, so I didn't mail the form. Never heard another word, but Rick kept calling me to see if I had been violated and offered that he had, and said his lawyers were working on it.

A year later, I got a certified letter from the FAA with a postmark of June something, but the letter inside dated December, stating that I had my license suspended for 90 days. The back of this letter had some fine print about a proposed violation hearing and other procedures. Finally, if I appeal this violation, it stays the suspension until the final hearing. I called the number on the letter, which directed me to Mrs. Mays at the FAA legal department at LaGuardia Airport, New York. I was able to get through to her and explained my situation. I told her that I thought something was fishy with the back dated suspension letter. "Now now, Mr. Curry, let us see if we can work something out." I said that since the letter stated the suspension started December 31, that as far as I was concerned, the suspension was over being as it was now June. She told me that it doesn't work that way since I hadn't surrendered my license. I asked if the letter was sent in June, how would I know to send the license in

113

December? Then I asked if I had been stopped or ramp checked, would that suspension be in effect? She said she couldn't answer that. Next, Mrs. Mays said, let's see if we can work this out. How about if we change the suspension from 90 days to 30 days? I said I don't know; something just is not right; how come I didn't get the proposed violation hearing? In the violation, the FAA had thrown the book at me, with about ten things that can be tacked on any violation like reckless endangerment. Kind of like speed greater than reasonable, what is reasonable? In a storm, 5 mph could be greater than reasonable. Most of these violations are erroneous in nature and can be applied to any situation. Then Mrs. Mays asked how about removing all the violations except that you didn't have your license in your precession. I responded, that's okay, but still, something is not right. Mrs. Mays then asked, is there a time you don't use your license, like on Saturdays and Sundays, that you could lose your license? I told her that I have to fly every day in the summer season, so Mrs. Mays said, how about if you lose your license for not having the license on your precession for 30 days in the month of December? Just about that time, it hit me, I am dealing with the FAA, and I was never going to walk away unscathed; it's not going to get better than this, so I agreed.

In asking around, I was told that this Rick guy had been flying a plane that had some unapproved modifications. The FAA had told him not to fly it until he straighten out the paperwork, and that he had gotten caught flying it like three times. I know one time with me and another leaving Bob's, the engine quit, and he crash-landed in a cornfield. Through the grapevine, I heard that the FAA wanted to suspend him, and as he took it to court, they couldn't violate him without violating me. In hindsight, my plastic bag sealed with a copy of all my licenses was in the dumpster with the old seat rather than the plane. I found out that the waver certificate on Bob's wall only applied to over open water and not over land where a thousand feet of altitude is required. So I guess I wasn't totally innocent.

Around Thanksgiving, I mailed my license off. In the first week of December, I got a call from Zachery Bergman from the FAA legal department. "Mr. Curry, you were supposed to send us your license December 1st." I replied that I sent it in weeks ago, and I had a receipt from the certified mail. Mr. Bergman said, let me check, and I'll call you back. He did call me back and said he found it, no problem. About a week later, I answered the phone, and it was Mr. Bergman. "Mr. Curry, you were supposed to send us your license December 1st." At this point, I just couldn't help myself and responded, "Zachery is that you? You just called me last week and found it".

"Oh, okay, Mr. Curry, no problem." Now I was really getting concerned. "Wait, don't hang up," I said. Just exactly how do I get the license back; do I have to make a request, have an interview, or take a test or something?" He answered, don't worry, we will send it to you. I thought, great, and they don't even know they have it. A few more days went by, and the license showed up in the mail; it was only halfway into December.

Every time I upgrade my license or apply for something, I have to check the block that says I've been violated and go into this lengthy explanation. The FAA inspector in charge of my mechanic's license said that he checked on my violation and couldn't find any record of it, but since you can get in big trouble for not divulging or lying on the forms, I always check that block. Still, to this day, I don't know how this stands.

Chapter 8
Still In The Game

I had started my first year just totally consumed with wanting to fly every minute of every day. You might say "just eaten up with it." By the time the season was over, I had flown over six hundred hours crop dusting, with another three hundred and fifty pulling banners, and with a handful more hours dropping skydivers. I landed the Ag Cat on my driveway and with a lot of effort put the plane in the workshop attached to the barn near the farmhouse that we rented. The landlady rented me the workshop for seventy-five dollars a month, just a few hundred feet away from the house. The workshop was just big enough for the plane, with only a foot to spare all the way around, after the elevators were removed. I had made dollies for the front wheels out of 4x4 with four swivel wheels each, then jacked the plane up and slid them under the wheels so that I could maneuver the plane sideways. I had to pull the plane straight in on sheets of plywood that I laid on the ground, with the engine tight against the doorpost, and then swing the tail around with the elevators removed so the tail would just go through the doorway. Then push the plane sideways inside, being careful to miss the support post in the middle.

After all that flying, I did not desire to fly one more hour or even think about it until the next springtime. When I started, I thought that all I had to do was fly the airplane, which was pretty much true for towing banners. However, it seemed like for every hour flying, I would have twenty hours of groundwork for the crop dusting operation.

I have had quite a few people tell me how great it must be to follow your dreams and to fly all day, buzzing around farms and come and go as you please, but I answer them with this question: what is your hobby or favorite thing to do? For instance, say you love to go fishing on your days off or on vacations, do you sit in your office cubical dreaming of the day you will quit your day job and buy a charter fishing boat just to fish all the time?

But what you didn't realize is that for every minute you spend fishing, you spent one hour preparing and cleaning up, in addition, you have to go every day no matter whether it's too hot or too cold, too raining, too windy, too foggy, or even if you don't feel good. Then after the day is over, you can't just go right home because you have things to fix or get ready for tomorrow. So, what I am saying is, why ruin a perfectly good hobby? Sometimes I think I should have stayed at the pill plant making little white pills all week and had a really bang-up airplane for the weekends. Still, I realized I'd probably gone bunkers if I stayed locked in that building.

OVER the winter, I bought and installed a newly rebuilt engine that Chester Roberts gave me a good deal on. I painted the plane and fixed and adjusted many other things, traded in all the coat hangers and duct tape for new parts. The plane really looked sharp! I also ran the night shift at the pill plant full time and still managed to do some dusting business sales work. Running the night shift was great, as Gus, who used to be my assistant, was now my boss. At night only one assembly line ran. The rest of the place was empty, no one in the office, absolutely no stress; it was great just to be a grunt with little responsibility. The only thing was that I was given an all Mexican workforce, and none of them spoke English. On the side of the machine that ran the assembly line of a dozen workers was a big green button to start it and a big red button to stop it. I would look at the workers and say, "It's time to rock and roll" and push the big green button. After a while, the workers would say, "It's time to rock and roll" in their broken English with a Mexican accent when they saw me getting ready to hit the button. The night shift worked five, eight-hour days, and the day shift worked four, ten-hour days. One night Gus told me before he left, to slow down the line, that each shift we were making thousands more pieces every night than the day shift made with two more hours. We really weren't working too fast, but the workers didn't want to go slower because they would get bored. By my second week, they had hired a girl who could speak English, which helped, but we had already gotten everything down pat.

I got a call in April from an upset certified seed grower in the area where I had done quite a bit of seeding that first year, so I rushed down there and met the farmer right before dusk. He showed me a trail of rye going right through the middle of his certified wheat field. With the sun skimming low across the top of the wheat field, it wasn't hard to see the scattered rye trail about eight inches taller and a thousand feet long with a gentle curve pointing towards the Crisfield Airport.

There wasn't any denying it. It looked like my work. In thinking back to last fall, I remembered that before I started Coulbourne's couple thousand acres of cover crop, which I had led him to believe I had done "lots of times before." I figured the best way to get started was to do a small job of thirty acres first. The field was divided into thirds by ditches. I decided the best way to start my new career in cover crop application was to calibrate the plane using this smaller field, before I started Coulbourne's large job. I carefully poured just the right number of seed bags into the plane for ten acres. On the first flight, the seeds came up light, on the second flight, I put them on a little heavy, and on the third flight came out just right. So with that, I looked behind the wings and didn't see any more seeds coming out, then looked in the hopper window. It looked empty, so I left the gate open, spun the stop back to keep the calibration. Satisfied with the planes calibration I made a gentle turn and headed back to Crisfield, not knowing this field was next to a certified wheat field.

I asked Kent the certified seed grower, what I could do to make this right? He told me that I could pull it all out, or that they could harvest that part as regular wheat, and I could pay the differences between seed price and regular wheat, or lastly, we could spray that area with Roundup, and I could pay for the lost crop. I replied that it was his field and that we would do what he thought best. But he wanted me to make the decision and stated that he had to finish spraying with his ground rig before dark and would I come back in the morning to talk it over.

Just getting started, I had never had such a problem and was extremely upset. I talked it over with Kay that night and decided the best thing to do is pay him to spray it with Roundup and pay for the acres. This way, it would all be resolved right away, giving satisfaction to the farmer, instead of risking any kind of elevation of a dispute. When I showed up at his home the next morning, he wasn't there, but his father was, and boy was he mad! He unloaded on me with both barrels; I didn't say a word. Thank God his wife was there and intervened. "Now Barney, we have all made mistakes." After he simmered down some, he asked what I would do about it. I replied that we would like to pay you to spray it and pay you for your loss. With that, Barney said that he had already spent too much on the crop and wanted me to go pull all the rye plants out.

I was so upset I went right away in the rain and started pulling the rye out. It took two and a half days, I had blisters from pulling out the wet plants. To my dismay, when I stopped back the next week, most of it was back. The plants that I had pulled up and thrown aside had regrown and turns out that it is necessary to carry the plants away from the field. So, I went back weekly until harvest, fearing if the inspector didn't pass this field, I could be responsible for the whole thing. By the end, I was cleaning up some mixed variety wheat that really was the grower's problem.

Somehow lemonade was made from my lemon! I thought for sure I would be the laughingstock of the area farmers and just be thrown right out of the county. But this seed grower could be a little abrasive, had a reputation for being difficult to deal with, and was noted for suing most anyone for anything. Being the only seed grower in the area, most of the farmers begrudgingly had to deal with Barney and were sympathetic to my plight; if anything, it helped business. I must say Barney was very fair with me, and after watching me pull the rye, and with my periodical reports, he decided that I was okay. The next year he gave me quite a bit of spraying. I still have to put up with the occasional farmer joking around, like the farmer who told me he had a bucket of rye seeds and was going to spread them along the edge of Barney's field as they drove by and then tell Barney they saw my plane down there.

ONE spring morning I had to spray a field near the Snow Hill VOR, (VHF Omni Directional Range Radio) a big white thing about ten feet tall sitting on a small building, looks like a big bowling pin, and emits radio waves for aircraft navigation. This VOR is about a mile and a half outside of NASA's Wallops Island Flight Facility airspace. Normally as I got to the area, I would call them on the radio, as required to enter the area, and even call them if I was just near the area but not in it. As I tried to call, it became clear that I had grabbed the wrong headset and couldn't transmit. My handheld GPS showed I was outside the airspace by about a half-mile, so I went ahead and sprayed the field. On one of my passes, pulling up pretty hard for the tall trees, a set of landing gear from an F-16 fighter crossed right in front of my windshield not much more than twenty or thirty feet away! Needless to say, it got my attention.

Later that day, I got a call from Wallops wanting to know if I had been in their airspace that morning; I answered that I had been near their airspace but did not go in it. The guy insisted that I had busted their airspace and said the pilot of the F-16 was really upset. I answered, "Upset, who do you think would fare out the worst if the two of us had tangled?" Now starting to get my dander up, I told him that I hadn't erased my bread crumb trail on the GPS and would bring it down there for him to see. Then he asked what my tail number was; I replied six o one Yankee. He answered, oh yes, we talk to you all the time. I explained that the radio had quit, and knowing that I wasn't in their space, I proceeded to do the job. Then I added that I wondered if they weren't shooting approaches on the VOR and then milking it in a mile or so into their airspace? After that, he decided to drop the issue.

GORDON had bought a King Air for his sky-diving operation. I wanted to fly it, so I opened the latest copy of Trade-A-Plane, and on the center page, halfway up, I read an ad that said "Get your multi-engine rating in the heart of America, St. Louis $895." So, I signed up, jumped in the truck, and drove out there. The way this program works was the instructor spends the whole day training you in the things involved in the multi-rating, mostly turning off one engine or the other and all the procedures involved. No time was spent on the basics, and the instructor did the radio work and navigation to save time, since the check ride is only about the advanced rating. Then the next day, I would take the check ride with an examiner that is on staff. The morning of the check ride, when I woke up in the hotel room, my right eye had swollen up and swelled shut.

About a month earlier, a chemical hose had broken in the bottom of the plane in such a way it couldn't be turned off, creating a mist inside the cockpit. Even though I put the plane in a steep climb to make the chemical run out the back, and tried to put my head out the window, I still couldn't get completely away from the chemicals. Every few days after that my eyes would swell up, first on the bottom left eye, then the top left eye, then the next time the top right eye, then the bottom right eye; it seemed to travel in a circle every few days but was getting less frequent and I thought it was going away. But the morning of my check ride it was back in full force. I put ice on it and headed out to the airport.

When I arrived, they told me that the examiner who normally did the check ride test was sick and they had to call in another, and then they informed me he was a little tougher. When the guy showed up, we talked a little, and he was concerned if I would be able to function okay or that maybe I should come back when my eye was better. I was able to talk him into letting me try since I was so far from home. I could tell that he was going to be tough. I had heard stories of pilots going for an advanced rating and making a basic mistake like letting a tire roll one inch past the painted line and ended up losing their primary license. After we got situated in the plane, the first thing that happened was I had to get out and run into the terminal and buy a current chart and ask what the airport radio frequencies were, since the instructor had taken care of the radio calls the day before. The examiner gave me a really strenuous workout, pulling engines at inopportune times, doing go-arounds on one engine, and so on. He would pull an engine while I was going through shutdown procedures. He would say, "Give me a two hundred per minute climb to the right, roll out on fifty-five degrees, ten-degree bank, level off at twenty-three fifty." To be honest, I don't think I ever looked out the window; I was too busy looking at the gauges. After this intense workout, looking over at me he said, "That was satisfactory, I think I will pass you.

Now head on back to the airport."

Finally, I was able to look out the window, but I still wasn't familiar with the area. (Hell, I didn't even know what side of the Mississippi river I was on.) I just knew that if I couldn't find the airport, he would fail me. So, after looking around, I could see some kind of major highway off to the left. I told the guy that my eye was really bothering me, then pointed at the highway and said, "I can't really tell, but I think that's the runway right down there." In a panic, he spouted out, "No, No. It's over there near the blue water tower," and pointed off to the right. I found the airport and passed the check ride.

When I returned home that next Friday, Gordon asked me to go to North Carolina and bring the King Air back from the maintenance shop. I told Gordon that I really should get a little training first since I didn't have any turbine experience. Gordon made a call, then came back and told me that Paul, the guy in charge down there, would go around the patch with me before I would fly it home. Gordon felt that if anybody could fly a taildragger, they could fly anything. I was just nuts enough to do it, but the only reason I didn't was I had about a seven-thou-sand-dollar day lined up spraying wheat.

A few weeks later as I was getting some King Air training with Mark, the pilot who flew jumpers on the weekends. While flying jumpers, Mark told me when the jumpers are exiting, they like to gather at the door, so they can jump together. When they gather up, they block the airflow over the tail section. "You will really have to stomp the rudder to keep the plane straight." I did just what he said, and three or four jumpers shot off to the left, and the rest jumped back in the plane and wanted to know what went wrong? Evidently, Mark was not a tail wheel pilot, and his idea of a lot of rudder, was a lot less than I was used to. In fact, the Ag Cat really doesn't have enough rudder for the maneuvers used in ag flying, and often you have the pedals buried against the floor wanting even more. So I may have overdone it, but he did say stomp it. Mark was really decent about it and told the jumpers that we just hit some air turbulence.

I was getting really proficient with the plane, and then the 9/11 happened. Skydiving died off, and Gordon was forced to sell the plane. The plane was expensive and had to do so much each week to make the payment. Gordon was something else, he was 80 and still going strong, making jumps himself weekly, running the jump zone with everything that goes on; it's like a circus atmosphere all day long. There didn't seem to be much money to be made, but he kept things going hand-to-mouth, just because he loved it.

One other time Gordon asked me to go to North Carolina and bring back the King Air and that he would fly me down. So we loaded up in a Cessna 182 jump plane with only a pilot seat, and I sat on the floor. Halfway over the widest part of the Chesapeake Bay, Gordon had requested flight following. They gave him a transponder code. Gordon fumbled with putting the numbers in, giving it his full attention. In the process, the plane made a complete 360 degree turn and lost a thousand feet. And he was totally oblivious to this. I sat on the floor, trying to fig-ure out at what point I should no longer care about hurting Gordon's feelings and take over. Finally, he got the numbers in before we got too close to the water, looked at the handheld GPS, and announced that we were still right on course, never noticing the 360 turn or the missing thousand feet. I couldn't help but think back to my youth when I would watch a cartoon,

"Mr. Magoo," driving his car through, over, and around all kinds of things, totally oblivious to his surroundings.

POWER lines and wires have always been a concern. The ones I hate are called sleepers; they come out of the woods and go across the field and back into the woods without poles in the field. For the most part, I depend on the telephone poles to find where the wires are.

The first pass of this particular field was along the woods to the right side, heading east, looking straight ahead into the morning sun flying a foot or so over the crop. As I approached the corner, preparing to pull up, there was a set of wires, green in color, same color as the trees in the background, just to fool a duster. I had no choice but to pull up into it, as there wasn't enough room to go under before the trees. When I pulled up into the wire, it snapped on the left side, but got wedged in the gap between the N strut and wing, making sparks like a welder and leaving a big black spot on the right wing. When the wire took up, the plane made a quarter turn to the right, and I was now facing south. But the wire had broken at the right pole, and I was still flying, trailing about one hundred foot of wire. I finished the job, being sure to come in high over the power lines along the road so the trailing wire wouldn't touch them. It was a busy day; I didn't have time to fool around, I landed, pulled up to the pumps, and climbed on top of the plane. Kay gave me the gas nozzle and I began to fuel up. A farmer pulled up to leave some chemicals, and at the same time, Kris our grandson stopped by. I yelled down to Kris over the running engine's noise to get some cutters and cut that wire off my wing. I finished pumping gas and chemicals in the plane and took off. The farmer was amazed and asked Kris if I cut down power lines like that all the time.

BREAK your own rules and it'll get you every time. I was taught to circle every job first, looking and familiarizing myself with obstacles and hazards, even if I had been there ten minutes ago. I had flown this field many times and felt that I knew it, but being in a hurry, I elected to just jump right in rather than waste time circling, not realizing that I had only ever done dry work like seeding or fertilizer there and had never been low enough to see everything. Diving in on the first corner, I caught a glimmer of something shiny, a wire in the sunlight cutting across the corner with no poles in sight. I yanked up hard, but still hit the wire with the landing gear, and the chemical pump. It didn't damage the landing gear which broke the wires, but it did rip off the pump. Unfortunately, I was spraying Dimethoate, which stinks like rotten eggs. With the hoses ripped out of the pump, the emergency dump door somehow triggered, the stuff went everywhere. The whole plane stank! It was about a ten- or a fifteen-minute ride home with that nasty smell. I could see the shadow of the pump hanging down below the plane as I landed, but there was nothing I could do but land and let the pump bounce along the runway. If the pump hadn't been banging into the runway, I think there would have been very little damage; still, it wasn't too bad, just broken plastic blades. It was a quick fix. I keep extra blades because sometimes the weeds will hit them and break them off, mostly towards the end of the season, when the weeds are tall.

Typically, the power company charges two to three hundred dollars to put the lines back up. This time the power line was a little bigger, and they wanted almost four thousand dollars. Maybe the line crew was pissed for having to smell that rotten egg stink. When I protested the amount, they wouldn't bend, but they did put me on the easy payment plan for a year.

FOR the most part, I abide by my own rules and circle every job looking for hazards. There are not any Amish farms in my area, so I know every farm has an electric service. I always establish where the electric service is. Can I see wires and poles or maybe a gray conduit pipe going up a pole along the road indicating underground service? I have a few farms that still have telephone poles, but all of the wires have been removed, and I know they're gone, but I still can't bring myself to fly through them. Hunters around here often will string up small wires for dove hunting that are hard to see, but for the most part, small wires like phone lines and cable TV normally don't hurt the plane much.

PEOPLE are always asking me if I am afraid that something might go wrong. In fact, the time I was most afraid, nothing actually happened. This watermelon field that I sprayed weekly was L-shaped with a dirt road running along the L's long side, leading to the L's short side. This was probably my third time to spray it this particular morning. I took time to circle and look things over. The long irrigation was pretty much out of the way, up against the dirt road with a chicken house behind it, but the short irrigation system was going caddywhoppist across the middle of the short side of the L. Since the long end of the L was much wider, I moved a couple passes over from the dirt road and started spraying down the long end, making a racetrack pattern coming back in on the short side, hopping up and down over

129

the irrigation and up again for the chicken house. Around and around I went with the gravy run on the one side, and bobbing up and down on the short side. Finally, I had gotten done with the short side, and on the next pass I could just shoot along the dirt road the whole length. Feeling relieved the hard part was done, I just jumped in and started spraying with the right wing hanging over the dirt road. As I got ready to make the spray pass next to the chicken house that I had been pulling up for and now was planning to just stay down on the deck, I noticed a black pickup truck, and at the last minute decided to pull up so I would not get spray on the truck. As I pulled up, I saw a flash of something directly in front of me. It was the rusty colored end gun to the irrigation system that I had forgotten about sitting along the dirt road that I was getting ready to hang a wing over. I had barely missed it when I pulled up! I pulled up high and circled around, caught my breath for a minute before I jumped in and finished. In the next couple of days, I couldn't stop think-ing about how I was not even a half-second from having the end of that irrigation pipe smash through the windshield and my face! The moral of this story is that my reward for doing the right thing is that I am still here to tell you about it. The penalty for being inconsiderate is death by being speared in the face with a rusty 6-inch pipe.

I was told a story about a NASCAR driver who just had a hor-rific crash but climbed out of the disintegrated car without a scratch. A reporter interviewed the driver and asked him how did he survive such a terrible crash? The driver explained that he had installed a poor man's seat belt. The reporter asked him what a poor man's seat belt was? The driver explained that you bolt a

2 ½ ball hitch right in the middle of the seat, then you sit down over it; when everything goes to hell, your butt tightens up and holds you in place!

I had heard all the jokes about "I bet that really made your butt tighten up. "Now I am in my middle fifties, but I never had that experience and just thought it was something old men joked about. But one day I was down on the deck running towards a tall pine tree, once again judging the height of the tree by the width of the base, since the top wing blocks the view of the treetop. The tree was a lot taller than I anticipated. It looked as if I wouldn't clear it, and then it happened for the first time in my life I actually felt my butt tighten up.

ONE summer morning, I woke up a little earlier than usual. I don't know the reasons, but this day I just felt better than usual, even when I brushed my teeth at the old wall hung sink. I had to hold myself back from grabbing hold of it and just ripping it right off the wall, all because I felt some weird burst of energy. After taking a shower and feeling crisp and clean, ready to take on the world, I jumped in my pickup that was already hooked up to a load truck and headed to a borrowed private runway about twenty miles away. It was just getting light, and there were very few other cars on the road. I always love that feeling of being out and about, getting things done before the rest of the world is awake. Even to make that euphoria feeling better, I had time to stop at Hardee's and get my favorite beefsteak and cheese biscuit with mustard and pickles, a big event for me since I work out of the house and rarely get to stop for coffee on the way to work, as I had done for all my working years until recently. Adding to the day was that it was a smaller job to do, and not much else was going on, so I was just going along at a lackadaisical pace. I dropped off the load truck, headed home, and gave Kay the pickup to meet me over at the runway. I waited a little bit, then fired up the old bird, and headed over, taking my time, so I wouldn't beat Kay there, just looking around at the scenery, passing the Vo-Tech school where Kris attended. I would be working in sight of the school, it felt good to know he'd see me working, probably pointing me out to his friends.

As we positioned the farmer's trucks and load truck along with everything else needed to load the plane, it was warming up. Still no concern and no rush. They had delivered a truckload of urea fertilizer with some kind of coating on it for me to spread over the corn. Things were going great, even the runway was twice as long as needed, but it was taking a little longer to get done than what I had envisioned. No matter; nothing else to do. As the warm morning gave way to a hot afternoon, we started to have problems with the fertilizer clogging the load augers, but we managed to make it work. The hotter the day got, the more the fertilizer stuck together. Now I was having a hard time getting the stuff out of the plane and wondered if the wind-driven agitator that I had removed would have been helpful. The only way I could get the stuff flowing was to kick the hopper vigorously as I would start each run, which did work. However, on about my third flight of having to do all of that kicking, I suddenly developed a Charley horse leg cramp. Man, did that thing hurt! As there is no place to straighten out your leg, somehow I even managed to get my foot stuck in the framework next to the pedals. I just pulled up high and circled, maybe I yelled a little bit. It seemed like forever until the Charley horse subsided. Funny thing, I'm not a doctor, but I wonder if the nerves that feel pain pass through the voice box on the way to the brain, because it sure helps relieve the pain if you yell. It especially helps if you throw in some profanities. I still had a great day, but I'll have to admit that old Charley horse took the edge off it.

ONE Sunday morning, specifically Father's Day, while spraying watermelons, ka-bamm whoppa whoppa whoppa coupled with a lot of smoked, I was thinking, here we go again with another blown cylinder. I went ahead and landed in a fresh cut wheat field. It probably would have made it home, but uncharacteristically I decided to play it safe rather than cross over the river and a fair amount of woods. I walked up to the nearest farmhouse. After a little begging, and while I stood on the sidewalk with a little dog biting my pant leg, the lady called Kay to come to get me. After what seemed like an eternity, Kay came and took me home. I loaded the pickup with tools and a new cylinder, then returned to the plane. I backed up to the plane, for this was getting almost routine. While I stood on the tailgate swinging wrenches, Reggie Sellers Jr., a farmer that lived nearby, stopped by and asked "What's up?" While I talked to him, Josh Brinsfield, Balvin's son called him from church, and Reggie told him what I was up to. After church let out, about a dozen pickups full of people surrounded me with curiosity. This made it hard to make any time with the repair; however, I was able to borrow a couple wrenches that I needed from Balvin.

After getting the new cylinder on, I had to take off with still ¾ of a load, and just cleared the trees by just a couple inches to spare. I returned to the watermelons and finished the job. After returning home, I went to Bennett's airport to have a lively discussion with Bill about another duster using the airport, which turned out that the competitor had led Bill to believe he was helping me. Bill thought he was doing me a favor. I had to apologize for the lively way I presented my concerns. Anyway, after that, Bill didn't allow the competitor back anymore.

I rushed home, showered, and shaved, and rushed to our favorite Italian restaurant. I met my father in the foyer. He looked at his watch and commented that I was right on time, 2:00. I responded, "You don't even know what I have done to still be on time," and proceeded to explain my morning.

Chapter 9
9/11

Working off a small, short, abandoned grass strip in Somerset County, I would have to come in slow, almost too slow, over the tall pine trees, then shove the nose over, pointing straight at the ground, then round out inches above the grass, stopping just before the tall trees at the other end. The really tall grass and weeds helped to slow the plane. But the risk was worth it; the fields I was seeding were right across the street. I was making great time, about four to five minutes from takeoff to the next takeoff, never getting more than seventy-five feet high, just enough to clear the trees and the power line out at the road. Suddenly the farmer I was working for came over and told us the World Trade Center had just been bombed and that I wasn't allowed to fly. Thinking of the bombing in the Trade Center years earlier, mostly broken glass and smoke, I said that can't apply to us and went back to work. A little while later, the farmer came back and said this is for real. My thought was never had all airspace been shut down in the history of flight and that we are pretty far from any large cities, out in the middle of nowhere, no way this could apply to me, the farmer must be mistaken, so I kept flying. The next time I landed, Kay was visibly upset and told me that Wallops Island (NASA) called and said if I didn't quit flying, the military would shoot me down.

So much for all the times I would call ATC at a couple of thousand feet for traffic advisories while climbing up with the parachute jumpers, then shortly thereafter, an airline commuter would blow right by, with parachutes falling on each side of it! I would complain that ATC didn't call out the traffic, and they would say that I was too low to pick up on the radar. Yet, not even at treetop height, the radar saw me when they wanted to.

I left the plane on that makeshift runway next to an empty cornfield and headed for home. On the way I called my buddy Dave Hrupsa in Felton and told him that we couldn't fly. He answered, "What's that you say? I can't hear you over the engine; I'll call you back when I'm done flying." When we got home and turned on the TV, I understood what terrible thing had happened. After four or five days, they lifted the ban on flying. With the cover crop deadline fast approaching, we went back to work right away. I quickly finished the job where we had left the plane and started some fields around home, where I had quite a bit of work. Not long after we started working around home, Dave called very upset, saying that we couldn't fly again; apparently, while he was flying, a big military gunship pulled up beside him and pointed at the ground in such a manner that it was obvious that he needed to land right away! So, I answered, "What's that you say? I can't hear you over the engine; I'll call you back when I'm done flying."

A couple days later, flying my 600 Ag Cat, as I would come and go, I would catch a glimpse of my cherished Lite Frame Ag Cat tied down next to the area where we loaded the plane. Kay oversaw the ground crew and all of the activity taking place, with farmers, farmer's trucks, our trucks, seed carts, and equipment for loading the seeds. About midafternoon, as I approached the airport, something didn't look right about that plane, so after landing and pulling up to it, I could see that the right wings were hanging down on the ground. I turned off my engine and climbed out to see what the heck happened, thinking that George, who had been cutting the grass with a tractor, had hit it, but he wasn't anywhere to be seen. Strangely, nobody was around at all, when only minutes ago there was four or five people helping load seeds when I took off. I heard some teeheeing from Kay behind one of the tractor trailers. Then out came Kay and everybody else. She started in, "We all hid because we knew you would blame us, but the thing just went ka-boom, and nobody was even near it."

A day earlier, I had hit a power line. Once on the ground, I looked the plane over, everything appeared to be okay, except for a small mark on the wing's leading edge, so I didn't think much of it. But when I looked at the broken landing wire that holds the wings up, you could see two hard bends that must have been made by the power line. When the landing wire was in tension, the bends didn't show. I believe that as the sun heated up the plane, the wings expanded enough to stress the landing wire that was already in tension to break.

The next day after finding the broken landing wire, the local TV station wanted to interview me about the terrorist attempt to use crop dusting planes to spread anthrax. I wouldn't agree to help them hype up the anthrax thing, but I agreed to do an interview about the hardship caused by the flying ban. The interview worked; I said that the state was unwilling to extend the seeding program deadline when the government was the one who took away the days. After they left me, they interviewed one of the congressmen that had voted down the deadline extension and asked what he was doing to help the farmers. The very next day in a reversal, he voted for an extension. Nobody ever noticed the 55-gallon drum under the wing holding up the wings during the interview or on TV.

The next day a woman from the FBI came by to talk to me about terrorists stealing ag-planes. She seemed a little surprised to find out that most planes of this type don't use keys. I assured her that ag-planes were tricky enough to fly and that not everybody could fly one. Then I assured her that we are a close-knit community and strangers really stand out. Besides, if the guys down south ever got hold of someone fiddling around with their planes, you probably would find them at the bottom of the bayou with a set of cement shoes. She didn't bother me anymore.

I really wasn't sure I wanted to include writing this because this event took place due to sheer stupidity rather than just circumstances, but what the hell. A couple of days after the flight ban had been lifted, I had been flying off a cornfield trying to make quick work out of five hundred acres in a remote area near the bay. We had made good time and were almost finished when darkness set in, so I filled the plane up with seeds to weigh it down because a storm was coming that night, and left it there, hoping to finish the next morning. In hindsight, I should have flown home and tied it down.

It rained five inches that night and into the next day, but

finally, after three o'clock, the sun came out. John, a fellow duster who was helping me in Somerset County, and I were riding
around in a pickup checking out some fields. At one point, I
told John that we needed to hang it up for the day and just go
to the crab house down the road and eat some crabs and have a
beer or two. But I let the pressure of being behind and the state
deadline get to me and decided to finish that job so that all the
equipment could be moved that night. That way, the next morning, we could run full force at the next location without having
to stop and move.

The field we were using had ditches with trees growing up
in them, with one ditch splitting the field in half and one across
the end, like a big T-shape. But I never noticed that the trees
at the end on the left side were four or five hundred feet closer
than the right side that we had been using. Surveying the muddy field, it looked like the right side where all of the corn shucks
had been blown away by the prop blast was covered with standing water puddles. The left side still had all the corn stubble and
looked like it had absorbed the rain, so I opted to take off on
the unused left side. In the flying world, they teach you to pick
a point midway down the runway; if things are not just right by
that point, you can pull the power and safely stop before the end
of the runway, but beyond this point you may not be able to stop
before the end. This is called the decision point.

In this case, the decision point is where I applied the power
since the field was too short. The plane was loaded a little more
than usual because I had loaded it down in fear of the storm. As
I pushed the power forward, the plane slowly started moving; by
the time I got ¾ down the cornfield to the area where the farmer
had started plowing the field, the plane was just getting ready to

fly, so I pulled back just a little to try and get the plane to fly in ground effect. For a little bit, this looked like it would work as the wheels skinned over the plowed area, which the day before was of no concern because it was white looking, hard, and dry, the wheels would just bounce off it, but now it was a dark looking muddy mess. Then the wheels settled down into the mud; I yanked back on the stick and got the plane up again; it waddled for a little bit than sank back down. Too fast and too late to stop, I chopped the power, but the trees were just a few hundred feet in front. I picked a spot between the trees. Well, the trees took the wings off, then the ditch took off the wheels. Because of the way the wheels hit the ditch, the plane flipped upside down and was now on fire. Luckily, I am slightly claustrophobic and had removed the left window; when the top of the cockpit crushed, I wasn't trapped. Bob and other fliers always get on my case because I don't wear a helmet, just a headset for the radio. I always tell them that I am a fat man in much more danger of heatstroke than crashing. I didn't have a helmet on, and I didn't get a scratch on me until I undid the seat belt and fell on my head.

Once out of the plane, the only thing I could do was scoop up all the spilled seeds and throw them on the fire. The onlookers were freaking out and didn't know what to do. Kay, my wife, quickly rummaged through the pickup truck toolbox and pulled out two fire extinguishers and gave them to the two hunters with four-wheelers that had been watching and told them to run them down to me. The hunters threw the extinguishers over the ditch full of water to me. I sprayed the first extinguisher and almost had the fire out; I just needed another little squirt, and it would be totally out. These extinguishers were the new-fangled kind that somehow pushes and turns like a pill bottle instead of just pulling the pin to use. Somehow in a panic, I managed to activate the first extinguisher with no problem, but now that I felt the worst was over and I wasn't running on autopilot anymore, I couldn't figure out how to make the second extinguisher work, even though it was exactly like the first. Finally, I got it to work and finished off the fire.

As I trudged back to the starting point where the trucks, equipment, and people were, I couldn't help thinking that the day before, I had given John a ride to this place in the hopper (the chemical tank). I thought he needed more air, and when I cracked opened the dump door, I could see all the dirt and chafe whirling around John through the tank window. After he stood there watching me crash, I wonder if he was thinking that he could have been in that hopper. I'll bet he will never ride in my hopper again.

Two guys had parked on the side of the road to see what was going on. They said they were with the local fire company and wanted to check things out. I told them that everything was under control with nothing to worry about. Noticing that more cars were pulling over, I explained that at this time, there was a heightened awareness of anything to do with airplanes. I couldn't afford to make a spectacle out of this, and I asked them to just leave, so they left. Sensing a real potential for a media frenzy, I sent Kris, my twelve-year-old grandson with a utility knife back to the plane to cut the tail number off the rudder, which he kept, and has hanging on his bedroom wall even to this day. Then I pulled a phone book out of the back seat of my pickup and on the hood of my truck was thumbing through numbers for a roll-back tow truck so that I could get this mess out of there quickly, hoping not to get caught or in trouble by the FAA. Since 9/11, the FAA was violating anyone for anything, even if your wheel stopped one inch over a hold line. I found a rollback operator that would come help me out, and I had him agree not to come until after dark. The guy was great; he even allowed us to pull his truck through the mud with the farmer's big eight-wheel tractor to the accident site and back out. He really was great; from now on, I'm going to use him for all my wrecks!

While I was thumbing through the phone book, I heard the fire whistle go off in the distance, and then a whole fire company showed up, including the two guys that I had sent away. The plane wreck was hard to see behind the trees at a thousand or so feet away. With my other Ag Cat sitting behind us, everybody was drawn to our location. When the fire chief asked me what happened, I almost bit his head off, explaining that I had sent the two bozos away and that I couldn't afford to lose my license over a couple of guys that wanted to rubberneck. The chief explained that he was required to check it out since they were there, but if everything was safe, he would have them leave right away, and he did.

No sooner had the firemen left, and all of the cars that had pulled along the road drawing attention started leaving, here comes a county sheriff police car, and a woman cop gets out and asks what is going on. So, I explain that I had just spun out in the mud, everything was okay, that I would have it fixed in no time, and in this 9/11 time, I was concerned that the TV stations would blow anything to do with aircraft way out of proportion, making tons of problems, possibly jeopardizing my license, so I was trying to keep a lid on it. She was good about it, but while we were talking, a young deputy pulled in behind her; he got out and told the lady cop, who was obviously his superior, that he caught two guys riding four-wheelers on the road a couple miles back and told them that they were not allowed to do that. She told him that he was right and sent him back to check on the four-wheelers. He was totally oblivious to my plight. As she left, she explained that since this had been on the emergency radio, the state boys would probably show up.

Sure as hell, the state police showed up next, so again I went through the story of how I had just spun out in the mud, I would have it fixed in a jiffy, and everyone is making something out of nothing. As I was carrying on, they kept looking over my shoulder at my other Ag Cat. Finally, they said it looked okay to them, and they left. About ten minutes later, they reappeared, "Now come on, what's going on?" Then I pointed across the field at the patch of yellow behind the trees and explained that's the plane that had spun out and that I had probably cut a tire on a corn stock, and still would have it fixed in no time. The plane was far enough away and behind trees, it was hard to tell what you were looking at. From that distance, the bottom wings could look like top wings, and they didn't want to go through the mud, so they bought my explanation. They did ask me for my name and the tail number of the plane in case they had to do a report, and then they left. I still can't believe they never noticed I gave them the number off the plane they were standing there looking at!

That night we took everything home and piled it up behind the old chicken house and covered it up with tarps. That next week all the local fliers kept circling my farm looking for a wreck but never found it. About the middle of the week, the FAA stopped by and said that they heard I had a mishap and wanted to see what was going on. They looked at my other Ag

Cat, for which they had been given the tail number and I now was using. Next, they checked out the tire I showed them, which was an old tire I found that I had covered with mud and cut with a knife. They were satisfied that everybody was making a bunch of hooey out of nothing. After everybody was gone, I was just left with a pile of twisted, bent-up sheet metal that had once been a beautiful, recently rebuilt Ag Cat with a fresh engine, bright shiny new paint and had once been worth quite a handful of dollars.

Chapter 10
Sour Grapes

Got a call from Albert, the state pesticide compliance officer. "Tim, we have a complaint from a lady that you have sprayed her little boy with some kind of poison." If that didn't get my attention, I don't know what would. Taking this very seriously, I asked where? Then he told me on the river next to Chesapeake Nurseries. Now I was getting worried that maybe I had done something wrong, since I had been working in that area. Chesapeake Nurseries was a good customer, and I did work for them often. However dry fertilizer was the only thing that I had done for them recently. Next, I asked Albert what date? Since I also kept records by dates, I could look it up. Albert said he had a list of dates. Right then I realized this was a bogus complaint, so I couldn't help myself and answered, "Do you know the last time I went down there? I had to circle for forty-five minutes before that little boy came out, so that I could spray his ass." I knew I had another city slicker on my hands who was simply writing down the dates anytime she heard a plane. We are getting more and more people moving into the area who are unfamiliar with the agriculture process. City people want to have beach homes, but they can't afford beach prices, so they buy a little more inland, often next to farms. Most of these "city slickers" are from Baltimore, so we refer to them as Baltamorons.

IN the same area, Albert got a complaint that I had poisoned some ladies well, but the lady screwed up when she gave Albert the well report showing high nitrates, which everybody has in this region and didn't come from an airplane. The report was dated a year before I had even started in business. Ever since 9/11, people have become oversensitive to the low-flying aircraft. Recently in a small town nearby, someone reported that a small plane had sprayed something over the town. Fearing this could have been some kind of poison, they closed that area to the public and had all kinds of specialists running around in white Tyvek suits taking samples and testing everything, costing a ton of money, only to discover the white powdery substance was bird poop.

I am your best friend, and you don't even know it, is what I like to tell those who have been taught that the aerial applicators are poisoning the world. Every time there is a story about pesticides, the media flashes a picture of a spray plane, even if it is about the termite guy spraying under a house. For the most part, the chemicals used today are highly regulated and designed to break down quickly. One of the most popular insecticides is actually a derivative of natural flowers that have been known to repel insects. Applied by aircraft often, only 1 ½ ounce is used to an acre, leaving a very light mist on the crop or your fruit, where it can easily be wiped off. This light mist doesn't run off the plant, and stays on the plant until sunlight breaks it down. I would challenge anybody to take a teaspoon of anything and spread it evenly over their back yard. Only a plane with speed can apply such a small amount per acre.

SOME of the bad press we receive is understandable after watching the old films of vintage aircraft spreading a cloud of dust over everything and everywhere. Recently I was watching a documentary film about early flight and the plane was spewing out a white cloud of dust over top the bystanders, cars, buildings, horses, and anything else in its path. Some of the stuff coming out was really bad stuff, but that was the stone age. Now the spray is applied with GPS precision, by specially designed spray nozzles; even NASA got involved in designing aircraft dispersal systems. Think of the happy homeowner who sprays the weeds in their front walk according to directions, later unhappy with the results; then what do they do? They dump the whole container on it. We are highly regulated professionals who often get audited at least once a year or more. We have a lot of money tied up in expensive aircraft and related equipment, not to mention all the training and time. For most of us it has taken years if not a lifetime to get to where we are. We can't afford to lose our livelihood or everything we work for, and we can't and won't just dump the whole container on it as the above homeowner or the aggravated farmer might do. We are all aware that every time we take off, hundreds and hundreds of people watch us throughout the flight; why would anyone of us risk even one drop of pesticide getting in the wrong place?

For many reasons, airplanes don't spray as much as they

have in the past. Some think that they have done a great service by getting planes banned from spraying crops with that light mist that stays on the plant, but think it is quaint to watch the tractors work the fields, even if the ground sprayers are putting many gallons (normally 20 or more) per acre, some of which does run off and get in the ground. In some of the areas with a lot of homes encroaching, the farmers have had complaints about the spraying, so they have resorted to pumping the chemicals through the irrigation systems with thousands of gallons of water per acre, so as not to be noticed. Now how much more of these chemicals are likely to reach the groundwater that we drink? More and more trickle tape and other types of water lines are buried neatly in rows. Now with GPS, they can plow and plant missing these lines, and they pump the chemical through them, which is delivered through the root system into the plant. Now you are eating the chemicals in the crop and can no longer just wipe your apple off and safely eat it like you did when the plane sprayed it. Since the chemicals are being pumped into the ground, I am pretty sure some are heading for your drinking water.

Because of the pressure put on the produce growers by well-meaning environmentalists, large numbers of growers have quit. Now, massive amounts of produce come from other countries. Many of these countries have little or no pesticide regulations; some of them spray stuff outlawed many years ago in the USA. Why would some want to use banned pesticides? In some cases, the older formulas lasted much longer, so they worked better at killing whatever insects or fungi. The newer generation chemicals will break down for our safety, but this means they may have to spray the crop more than once. So, what have these well-meaning people done? They have us eating food loaded with chemicals absorbed by the roots, or foreign produce with all kinds of poisons. We have some of the best pesticide regulations in the world right here in the USA; work with them before you march and make me eat poison grapes from South America, when I could have eaten locally grown produce that I simply wiped off the pesticides.

Don't for a minute, think that I am an anti-environmentalist. I just wish more of the well-meaning environmentalists would really study their issues before marching to the cause, loaded only with the part that is sensational news presented by the media, or with the hearsay passed around, or especially through social media, on internet were every nineteen-year-old kid that has heard something or done something new thinks they are a genius and posts a YouTube video. Folks should remember that the experts and scientists more than likely publish their findings. Feeding the world and at the same time saving the environment is a complex issue. It's like trying to pull just one noodle out of a bowl of spaghetti without it touching another noodle. I am afraid that Mother Earth doesn't have many more noodles left to give us.

These numbers may be old, just go with the gist of what I am saying. Some feel that we should have only organic food; it's my understanding that with the shrinking available farmland, each year the average American farmer feeds 300 people and that an organic farmer feeds about four. How is this going to work? The population is only getting bigger. Maybe if each farmer shoots 296 people, it will work out. As little as 70 years ago, all our food was organic, and the life expectancy was about 45, should we go back to that? Seems lately, there are many E-coli and other recalls on organic lettuce, tomatoes, and other vegetables, but not so many recalls on the ones that are treated. Currently the pesticides are crucial for the farmers of the world of feed the ever-growing population. Some people trying to protect the environment have had aerial spraying banned in some USA counties, but that has inadvertently caused me to eat foreign poisoned fruit shipped from lesser regulated countries.

Have we been sold a bill of goods? People think they have done great things by buying a hybrid car, only to have done much more harm to the earth by the digging of huge copper, nickel, lithium, and zinc mines, along with the other resources used to make these batteries for hybrid cars, and later the environmental damage from the disposal of the batteries. The harm to our environment is greater than if they burned fossil fuel. Or like ethanol that takes more energy to make than it delivers. I am not so sure that solar panels, with the materials used to make them and their limited life expectancy, will be a great environmental savior. Most of these panels are being made overseas and brought here by big ships polluting our oceans. I have always wondered how much pollution is generated by the airlines, to carry all the engineers, CEOs, and businessmen back and forth to China to make deals, give out trade secrets and give away our economy.

I am thinking that population growth would be a better place to take aim. We may inadvertently solve global warming and a whole host of other problems, such as the wars that us humans fight over the dwindling resources that the over-populated countries are eating up at an alarming rate. Before I climb off my soap box, let me back up a second, so you will not think I am some kind of lunatic. Organic food, hybrids, ethanol, and solar panels are all good ideas and as we continue with these things they will get better and better; they should be viable in the future. No doubt we need to keep trying. I am just saying, as in my metaphor, as you try to fix things by pulling on that one noodle, let's not inadvertently dig big holes in our earth and not with the child labor some foreign mines use, only later to pour that battery acid back on the earth, and let's not generate more pollution, making items that take more power to make than they produce, let's not make more pollution shipping things around the earth when we make or grow these things in our own backyard, like fresh vegetables.

I installed a chemical container flusher in the mixing station, so every bit of chemical goes in the mix and the container is clean. Then I save the containers and the state picks them up once a year to recycle them. Every time I flush out the plane or change tank mixes, it is pumped into the appropriate holding tank, only to be added to the next time the same type is sprayed, so there is never clean-out material to dispose of. Like most of us, I have a GPS made specifically for applying chemicals on farm fields, capable of automatically shutting on and off the application at boundaries, recording everything, including weather conditions. It also will apply a variable rate to work in conjunction with the farmer's data, so we only apply what is needed.

I couldn't help but notice a silver VW bug was driving all over the yard in a very irrational manner, while I was spraying a field with a home and pool in the middle of it. It took me a couple of passes to realize that they were trying to flash the headlights at me. Now sensing their dissatisfaction with me being there, I started turning off the spray many hundreds of feet before the yard. However, I kept on spraying the field and was not overly worried since I was just spraying Growers Fertilizer, a fertilizer which I believe actually was organic. Meanwhile the car kept driving around like a maniac. I always finish up with a pass across the ends, so as I swung around and dropped down along the road edge, and ahead of me just a little bit was this VW. I turned the spray off probably a good hundred feet before the car. I don't know what got into me, but I held the plane down a bit longer, passing over the car by just a few feet.

When I returned to the airport to load up to spray elsewhere, I told Kay, "You may get a phone call on this one," and explained about the car going berserk. A little while later, as I landed, I could see that silver VW parked next to the load area. After parking the plane, I shut it off, even though I normally leave it running if I continue to work, but it looked as if I would have to give this some attention. Before I could climb down off the wing, the lady was standing there giving me holy hell, trapping me on the wing.

As I mentioned earlier where I live has been slowly building up. We are close to Ocean City, and many city folks are moving in. Beach real estate is expensive; many buy inland and around the less expensive farmland. With all these folks who have never seen a crop duster, we get a lot of complaints. The FAA told me that they know what time I start the engine and what time I turn it off because the phone rings the whole time. I take the complaints seriously, and I always stop what I am doing and talk to them. If they call, normally I jump in the car and go see them right away. I don't call them. I find that disputes can escalate over the phone but normally can be resolved in person. I have a system that works reasonably well for complaints. I call it killing them with kindness. First, let them have their say, don't cut them off before they are done, just stand there and take it, let them run out of steam, and then just tell them that you are sorry that they feel that way. When they finally settle down enough that I can get a word in, I explain what I was doing, including why I flew that particular direction because of the wind and so forth. I continue on about how we determine the wind direction, the special nozzles we use, the GPS, type of chemicals, and anything at all pertinent to what I was doing. Next, I get their phone number and promise to call them ahead of time if I must spray near them in the future. Then I compliment them on their home, admiring the great view and surroundings, then I throw in, "Do you see many deer?" I then mention that I think listening to a noisy plane five or ten minutes a year was a pretty good deal to protect the terrific view that they have, and if they didn't allow all the operations necessary for agriculture, that instead of that great view, maybe they would be staring at someone's trash cans or storage shed and the backside of some home when a housing development moves in, because the farmer got tired of the complaints and quit. I have found that it only angers them when you mention the Right to Farm bill, which specifically mentions aircraft operations. But I tell them there is such a law and quickly add that I am not trying to hide behind it and that I want to be a good neighbor and work with them, even though I don't have to. After that, I continue to apologize, and so on and so on. By this time, they are normally trying to close the door and get rid of me, stating they have an appointment, there's something burning in the oven, thought the phone was ringing, or anything they could think of, and chances are they will never call again.

But this time, I really lost it. As the VW lady finally stepped back, allowing me to jump off the wing, I unloaded on her with both barrels. "The problem with people like you is that you move in here from God-knows-where, build a house right smack dab in the middle of a pristine piece of farmland, and then commence with complaining about all the farming operations that have been in use for a hundred years, and you won't be happy until you run every farmer out of business." I continued, "We have the best regulators and the most modern practices in the world right here in the USA. Since people like you have made it so difficult for the farmer, many have quit growing the vegetables that we eat, so now most of our vegetables come from South America, or God-knows-where, and they spray stuff that has been illegal here for many years. Every time I pick up the paper, I read about a ship detained in quarantine at some port with some kind of poison, insect, disease, or hazard." The lady's husband, who had been standing next to her, and had looked like he was going to come to her defense, saw the fire in my eyes and just silently took a couple steps back. As I stomped away, I turned back still in a huff and said, "You just think about that the next time you buy grapes."

At the moment, it felt good to say my piece; later, I felt lousy about the unprofessional way I handled myself and almost went to the lady's house to apologize for the way I delivered my point but not the point itself. But then figured that I might just stir things up. The danger for a Type A person is that a very valid point can easily get lost in how the message is delivered; unfortunately, I have learned this firsthand on a few occasions, mostly with my wife.

FINISHING up spraying one morning and running behind, I decided to just continue on in the spray plane to Bob's to pull banners for the day. I called Salisbury tower to transition through their air space. They approved the transition and asked my altitude, to which I replied five hundred feet. Sometime later, while I was getting the banner plane ready, one of the guys from the FAA showed up for a meeting with Bob, but when he saw me, he said, "I was in the tower this morning when you called in. You better fly higher, or you are going to get in trouble." I responded that I was over five hundred feet and over an agriculture area, and that was all that was necessary. He said, "No, you were over a congested area. As far as I am concerned, two farmers and an outhouse is a congested area." I think he could see the fire building up in my eyes as I struggled to come up with a response. Then he said, "See, what I mean? Only a judge will be the one to make that determination. Be careful."

Many years later, that congested airspace would come up. I was cover-crop seeding an area near the town that has been building up due to the college nearby. The FAA called and said they had a complaint. Turns out the complainer was a Baltimorean that moved down here and was three blocks away from the area I was seeding, but still sparked an investigation. Lately, the FAA has taken the attitude that anywhere within one mile of a building could be a congested area. The only rule that governs us is if you fly over a congested area, you must meet special rules like the plane must be within a hundred-hour inspection, you must file a flight plan with designated areas for emergency landings, and you must serve notice to the area before the flight, such as a radio announcement or newspaper.

After I was done for the season, I agreed to take my GPS

printout to show my flight path to the FAA office. We ended up with that conversation about the congested area. They felt that I was in a congested area, and I showed them that I was over farm fields all the time, and we argued for a bit. Finally, I said, "You tell me what an area is, and I'll stay out of it." Then added my wife told me that an area is a spot between my plate and the candle stick on our kitchen table. They responded that the "area" was in conjunction with congested. I questioned, "What do you mean by congested? Are you talking about congested heart failure or congestion on the L.A. freeway"? I continued, "The words (congested) and (area) are erroneous and have no value. The only word that has value in the rule over a congested area is (over). As far as I am concerned, if I fly next to the Empire State Building just about rubbing my wingtip on it, but I didn't go (over) it I didn't do anything wrong. Furthermore, if the stairways and elevators are not clogged up, and the people are moving around freely, it's not even congested, and I could fly over it."

I could sense some major frustration building within the guys I was telling this to. So I said, "Look, I'm not really that defiant, I was just making a point. You guys have picked out some imaginary border a thousand feet out in the middle of a cornfield and call it a congested area, which is not right. Why don't we compromise and call the road separating the cornfield and buildings the border?"

The FAA does not have a clear published definition of Over Congested Area that governs the aerial applicators. I believe that when the rules are unclear, you must look at the spirit it was written, or maybe what is the industry standard. In this case, two farmers and an outhouse would mean just about the whole country, so if you mean everything, why bother to make a rule

BOB had asked me to apply cover crop on a two-hundred acre field for one of his customers. The field was a rectangle with the long side running along the road leading right to the Bay. On the side towards the Bay was a row of homes between the field and the water, mostly summer homes. Bob had suggested that I could fly the field longways to make quick work of it. That would mean I would have to fly over the homes, so I elected to fly the field short ways, adding considerably more time to the job. As I made the first pass along the edge with the homes, I could see a man standing in his back yard next to some dog pens, waving his arms profusely. It was evident that he was unhappy with me being there. So, I maintained a couple hundred feet between me and the yards as not to get any seeds near the yards. Each flight, I would complete three or four passes, about thirteen acres, so it would take quite a few trips to finish the job.

Somewhere between my third or fourth trip, I received a call from the 911 service, stating that a man said I had sprayed his dogs with some kind of poison. He had them loaded in the car on the way to the veterinary, and he needed to know what I had sprayed and what was the antidote. I explained to the 911 operator that I had seen the guy and was nowhere even near him, and furthermore, I was only dropping wheat seeds. Then I added, "Do you suppose the dogs could get a yeast infection?" I never heard anymore.

SOMEHOW one of my favorite chemical dealers talked me into spraying a field with Roundup for a customer known to be hard to deal with. A few days after I had sprayed the field, I was doing a little more Roundup for someone else. While passing over this field, I looked for places that weren't turning yellow. Then

I touched up one or two spots, which made me feel that the job was well done. About a week later, the customer called and said he was unhappy with the job, so I agreed to meet him at the field. We both pulled in and parked on the dirt lane dotted with telephone poles and wires leading back to the farmhouse in the back. We were parked on the dirt lane under the big poles with heavy duty electric lines running along Route 50 and the field's edge. The guy pointed to a spot the size of my pickup's hood, underneath the intersection of these power lines and told me that I missed that spot. We were standing about twenty feet away from one of the tall poles in the field where the weeds were clearly dead from the Roundup. I pointed at that pole and said, "I went this far before I pulled up, how far would you had gone?" He saw my point, so I gave him a pocketknife with my company name printed on it and he was happy!

Chapter 11
Life Is Good Almost

Springtime, working towards my third season in business, I had built a hangar over the winter and even found time to paint up the 600 Ag Cat. Things were slowly getting more organized and falling into place. I had started building up a pretty respectable customer base. I could now afford to buy real airplane parts and do away with all the coat hangers and duct tape holding things together. Mr. Leary my FAA inspector called to set up an inspection. I was fortunate to have this inspector; he had started his career working on his uncle's Ag Cats and knew all about the ag business. He had worked his way up the aviation ladder, working on everything, including jets, eventually becoming an FAA inspector. He was down to earth and very reasonable, a man of integrity who was not going to allow me to do anything that wasn't right. I felt comfortable enough with him to ask any question I had without fear of retribution. I believe his approachable method ultimately made us much safer rather than the inspectors we all avoided. When I made the appointment, I wanted to show off my new hangar, and thought everything was in good shape. My only worry was cutting the grass.

While finishing up the hanger and with all the other things going on, I had fallen behind in getting my favorite Lite Cat inspections done and ready to fly. So, I had been flying the 600, spraying the wheat fungicide, which turned into a good amount of work. The 600 with a fresh engine was a good plane but lacked the Lite Cat's maneuverability and was heavy on the stick, my arm would be tired at the end of the day. A couple of rainy days came in, and I was able to finish the Lite Cat inspection, so I started flying that, and it felt great. On Memorial Day morning, I finished early about ten o'clock, and it looked as if all the wheat was now complete for the season. During that time of the year, the wind blows every day, constantly beating up the pilot and plane. That coupled with flying from sunup to sundown for a month and half, so I was a little burned out. I told Kay, who had been doing all of the mixing, that I was going to fly home, and just take the rest of the day off, watch John Wayne war movies and rest.

Who knows what goes through a man's mind? When I arrived home feeling great, since all the work was caught up, and I was flying my favorite plane, for whatever reason, I decided to land over top of the farmer's tractor parked on my taxiway with only about four to five hundred feet left, instead of landing on the runway, As I touched down a little faster than I should have, my thoughts went back to the time I ended up in Bob's ditch, so I decided this wasn't the best idea. Maybe I should just power up and land on the runway. As I pulled up, because of the speed, the plane began to climb right away. I must have put the power in too fast, "a-hught, a-hught" the engine just coughed a couple of times and did nothing, leaving me with the nose pointed skyward at about fifty feet above the ground with very little speed. I shoved the stick forward, to get the nose down. Now I was looking at the trees in front of me. I tried to turn left as not to go into the trees. Out of speed and everything else, the plane came down hard on the left wing. It bent the bottom wing so that it almost touched the top wing, straighten out the curve made in the left gear leg, knocked off the right gear, and bent the propeller. I had been pushing so hard on the left rudder pedal that the steel tubing holding the pedal was bent.

So now, my beautiful plane is reduced to a pile of yellow sheet metal in the middle of the taxiway that was easy to see from our driveway, and with the wheels gone, I couldn't move it. I wonder if anyone reading this could ever remember getting that first scratch on your new car or other prized possession, how upsetting it is. For it seems that the car is more than just an inanimate object, it's a living, breathing part of your life, and you don't think life will ever be the same with that scratch. This is how it is with a pilot and his plane. As I stood there scratching my head as to what to do next, I could see Kay's car coming down the driveway. The doctor had put Kay on high blood pressure medicine only a day before and had told her to avoid stress. I knew this is going to be a hard one to explain! Somehow I managed to stand next to Kay in such a manner to block her view of the plane, as I described the mishap. I may have understated the damage. I decided to avoid using the words accidents or mishaps (sounds so negative) and use the word experiences because, by now, I have had enough "experiences" that a funny thing happened. As I walked away without remorse or even a tear from the smushed up plane towards the shop to gather up tools, about fifty feet away, I looked back over my shoulder at the pile of twisted yellow metal of what was my favorite plane. Turning back towards the shop and without even missing a step, I asked myself "I wonder how much it will cost this time" and just continued to walk.

We had scheduled the FAA inspection for the next day, so now I was worried about more than just cutting the grass. First thing in the morning I called the Mr. Leary and asked if we could reschedule, that I had gotten too much work out of town. He told me that they had set up several other appointments on our side of the Bay, and it would probably be a while before they could come back again, that if it was okay, they would just stop by anyway and look around outside so he could check me off the list. After talking a couple minutes and finding out that they were inspecting Bob's first, we agreed that when they left Bob's, Bob would call me so I could fly back for the inspection.

Now that I could not get out of the inspection, I borrowed the farmer's tractor with a forklift front end and moved the plane behind the old chicken house and covered it up with a tarp. Around lunchtime, Bob called and said they are just leaving, so I flew back to the hanger and waited for them to show up. After a couple hours, they still hadn't shown. At that time, I was still loading and mixing out of Bennett's just ¼ mile on the other side of the tree line. I jumped in the plane and hopped over to Bennett's, then loaded up some chemicals to hit another job near Princess Anne, that was on the way back to Crisfield. As I took off, I notice what looked to be thunderstorms off to the west of my normal route. Hoping to beat the thunderstorm, I called Salisbury tower and got permission to go around to the east. Following the bypass around Salisbury, the storm caught up with me. The rain was so hard that the cars were pulling off the highway, and I was only a couple hundred feet above them. With the rain beating hard on the flat windshield, all I could see was straight down. The Ag Cat is not exactly watertight and I was getting soaked, so I radioed the tower and returned to Bennett's. Landing at Bennett's caught me totally off guard; apparently, the storm had passed through. I touched down in a huge puddle and almost flipped the plane; water shot everywhere including over the top wing. As I worked to keep control, down the runway near the gas pumps stood two guys in suits watching. As I rolled to a stop, it was Mr. Leary, my FAA maintenance inspector, and another inspector from FAA operations department. I asked them if they wanted to go over to my new hangar, but they said they were running behind and maybe some other day. The ops guy wanted to do a ramp check. The plane had just been all painted up, I had copied all licenses, medical and registrations, etc., and put them in a plastic bag under the seats of all the planes that I flew, so all my papers were in order. They were impressed.

A few days later, I moved the damaged plane into the hanger. The first thing I wanted to do was just get rid of the ugly crumpled up metal and get down to the unbent part. I wonder how many people reading this, have ever felt a presence of someone that was watching you from behind when you thought that you were alone? So, while I was cutting through the wing spar, I got that feeling. So when I turned around to see who was there, still holding the power Sawzall with a rough cutting 18-inch blade. It was Mr. Leary, the FAA inspector, standing there in amazement. "Oh my God what are you doing, what happened?" Lucky for me, Chris, Bob's young son, had run into his wingtip about a week ago with a Kubota tractor cutter. So, thinking on my feet,

I pointed over at the farmer's tractor and informed him that my grandson had run into the plane. I could see in his eyes that he didn't believe me, but he knew better than to pursue the subject.

LATE spring the year before, I still hadn't gotten the 600 Ag Cat out of the workshop. Noticing that the corn on either side of the driveway had shot up that week, because the farmer had applied nitrogen last week, I finally pulled the plane out of the shop. That was no small job. The wheels were on dollies, the plane had to be rolled sideways around a support column and swung out the door, before the elevators and rudder could be installed. After the plane was ready, I would tow it backwards with my pickup down the farm driveway to the road, then take off towards the farm. Normally I would go over the barn that was 800 feet straight ahead. With the empty Ag Cat it was not much of a problem. This time, the fast-growing corn was brushing the bottom wing, and I didn't think it was a big deal. I only worried about getting green stains on the wings. It is just unbelievable how much that corn kept the plane from getting up. There was no way I could get over the barn, at the last minute I was able to get up just enough to make a hard right bank and missed by a foot or two the windmill opposite of the barn.

CORN next to the runway is always a concern. Being a tight ass, I let the farmer that leases my place plant the corn right up to the edge of my runway, giving him more acres that I get paid for and less grass I have to cut. All summer long, my wingtips rubbed the corn, but I was careful, always on my toes. By late summer, the corn was drying down and sagging inwards more towards the runway, making the space even tighter. I was starting to get a little lacks since I had been in and out of the runway probably thousands of times trouble-free. One morning the masons showed up to start the foundation of my new home; I was busy flying and didn't have time to help get them started, so I was really watching them as I came and went. About my fourth time returning and looking down at them, it looked like they were laying blocks in the wrong place. I was paying too much attention to them instead of flying the plane. When I landed, my left wing just barely touched the corn, and the plane swung to the left. I stomped the right brake and rudder, pulled on the stick, but nothing worked to stop the plane from spinning. As it spun around and was now traveling backwards, all the pressure on the locking tailwheel plowing sideways caused it to snap off. Then the tailspring that had held the wheel dug in the ground like a boat anchor, stopping the tail instantly. The left window had been removed for years, and I ride with my elbow resting on the windowsill. I felt something hit my arm. When I looked, it was the tail end of the plane. The plane had snapped in half! Once again, there goes the year's profit.

PROBABLY the reason I was so lackadaisical about corn close to the edge of the runway is that I had gotten away with it many times before. Once at my friends Max's runway, when the farmer planted it too close, I managed to fly in and out all year several hundred times without a problem, but on one of my last days there, I sneezed while taking off, (did you know you can't sneeze without closing your eyes?) I felt the plane pull to the left, and I pulled hard to the right and pushed hard on the right rudder. I knew better than to look at the wing, just look straight ahead, and with full power, I got out of there. Once in the air,

I looked over at the left wing; there must have been a dozen corn plants bent over the leading edge. I shook, slipped, and rocked the plane, but it would never come off. When I landed and slowly rolled out, all of it just fell off.

ONE morning about nine o'clock, while I was down on the deck spraying a watermelon field, boom woppa woppa woppa. Then came the familiar oil all over the windshield. Here we go again, another blown cylinder. Thinking I'd like to have a nickel for every time I'd seen this movie. So, I pulled up, flew back home, and pulled right into the hangar. Having a lot of work planned for that day, I immediately started changing out the cylinder with the top blown off. By lunchtime, I had finished and went into the house to clean up and grab a bite to eat before going back to work. While eating my lunch, I turned on the 12:00 news just in time to see my friend John's plane upside down in a bean field. They were trying to flip the plane back right side up with his uncle's piece of heavy equipment while the news cameras recorded all of this. The plane was totaled; it looked like a limp dishrag as it flipped over. I found out, at just about 9:00, the same time my cylinder blew, the turbine engine on John's Ag Cat blew the turbine wheel, and the whole thing just came unglued right on the spot. With all of the engine parts leaving the plane, and nothing left to work with, he just barely made a bean field, and the plane flipped upside down. Luckily it was an Ag Cat, and John didn't get hurt.

I did want to point out that a sixty-or seventy-year-old round engine carried me home even with the blown cylinder, and just a couple hours later, after lunch, I started my engine up and went back to work. At the same time, the much younger turbine engine was dead. This many years later, that old round engine is still earning me and many others a living.

ON a hot, muggy summer night, my wife had been watching the 10:00 news and she told me that a thunderstorm was heading our way and I might want to put away the plane I left out. I was just about to turn in for the night. "Well, alright, I'll go put it up." We live on a farm away from anyone, so I just went out there in my underwear (tighty whiteys for anyone that just has to know) and climbed up in the airplane. Then I had to step on the narrow window edge in my bare feet, it was very uncomfortable, but I managed to get down in, start up, and swing the plane around facing the hangar door. Inside the hangar it was dark. I had forgotten to turn on the lights and by now the dark clouds and wind had arrived, making things that much darker. Thinking I really didn't want to step on that almost sharp window edge again, I told myself that it will be alright, I'll just pull in the hangar enough for the front wheels to get over the little bump in the concrete floor at the doorway and then just push it the rest of the way in myself. Normally in the light, I will taxi the plane all the way in, but I thought it would be safer to stop short.

Just as I pulled in, to my surprise BapBapBapBap metal went flying everywhere. I had just chewed the tail off my Cessna 182 which I forgot hadn't been pulled in all the way to its normal spot because I didn't want the whirling prop around the kids the day before when I gave the kids a ride. The worst thing is, all you want is for the prop to quit making that BapBapBap noise, however, the plane has no reverse. When you pull the mixture to shut down the engine, it still seems forever before the engine finally stops. I couldn't believe it; the prop didn't even seem to get a scratch on it. I was worried because it was Bob's plane. The Cessna didn't fare out so well; six or eight inches of both elevators, rudder, and tailcone were just gone. On the back of the tailcone there used to be a glass taillight no bigger than a thimble, and I found little glimmers of that glass for months from one end of the 120 foot hangar to the other. Later that year, when we went camping, I pulled down our RV awning, and more bits of white and green metal with shimmers of glass fell out.

Chapter 12
Good Ole Bob

R ight after Labor Day, Karl, one of Bob's banner pilots, went
to Texas to bring back a 600 Ag Cat that I had just bought.
My wife Kay made all the arrangements: hotel rooms, plane
tickets, etc. My mother arranged to get the money sent. This was
some years ago before everyone had cell phones and computers,
and the only way to get the money there was for Mom to charge
the plane on her credit card and for the seller's wife, who ran
a beauty shop, to retrieve the charge, (I'd sure like to have that
kind of credit card). For years Mom has bragged about how she
bought an airplane. They did all this while I was extremely busy
with a worm run (spraying worms that were destroying soybean
fields). I really needed the plane yesterday. Karl had only flown
my Ag Cat once around the airport right before leaving and it
looked like he would be okay.

I had jumped out of my plane between flying loads while
farmers who were standing around holding jugs of chemicals,
waiting to be next in line to get their field sprayed, were watching. I put Karl in the plane and talked him through a takeoff

and landing with a handheld radio. Then made him get out, and went back to spraying, while my wife briefed him on plane tickets and other details.

With our credit card in hand Karl was off to Texas. On his way home, he would call at night and give us his progress report. "Well, I had a really good day today," Thinking he would be in the Carolinas, I asked, "How far did you get?" Karl responded, "I made about a hundred and fifty miles, still in Texas." Now I was afraid I wouldn't need it by the time he got home, but in all fairness, he was new to the plane, and didn't have any mishaps.

I'd picked up several thousand acres of cover crop work near Bob's airport, and Bob had agreed to fly the 600 after Karl returned. Kay was jumping on the wing, flipping the lid, holding the shoot, closing the lid, and wiping off the windshield for both of us while her father drove the load truck. Bob told her that he didn't need his windshield cleaned, so Kay asked him, how do you see? He responded, "I fly with my eyes shut!" At the diner where we frequently had dinner after busy days, Kay said, "Do you know Bob flies with his eyes shut?" I thought that Bob was just being nice to Kay, not making her clean the windshield because Kay occasionally would overload him, causing Bob to get uptight. Sometimes it looked like he wouldn't clear the trees. Right before the trees, you would see some seeds shoot out of the plane, as Bob tried to lose some of the weight, and then he would just brush the treetops.

The next week Bob had to take a day off, so I thought that I would try the 600 since I had never flown one. When I pulled the handle to let out seeds, all this chafe, dust, and seeds came in the cockpit, swirling around, all in my face and eyes. I understood what he meant by flying with his eyes closed! The plane wasn't too bad, but it had a few issues, like the huge hole in the belly that let the seeds in and the fact that it burned more oil than an oil refinery. At the beginning of the week, Bob had bought a 55-gallon drum of oil for that plane, and by Friday, we were calling around looking for more. I figured out that if you buy a spray plane from certain parts of the south, rating the condition of the plane on a scale of 1 to 10, it will never go higher than 7. When you talk to the seller, for every time they use the word (clean) like "this is the cleanest plane in the county," take one point off on that scale, then you'll know what you're getting, somewhere between 3 and 4.

The next morning, I got an angry call from Bob. "You just don't understand when I fly for somebody, nobody else touches the plane." So, I asked what's wrong? "I went to take off and the engine quit. Someone turned the fuel off!" I just answered, "Sorry, but what happened to letting the plane warm-up" It must have been a hell of a preflight." In the 450 that I fly, the carburetor drips, so I'm in the habit of turning off the fuel every night.

Bob had agreed to help fly during the cover crop season. The only thing is that during the summer season, he works really long and hard, packing a whole year's work in just a few months. Every year he trains and manages a new batch of banner tow pilots, gives rides in his antique biplane up and down Ocean City beach, keeping about twenty airplanes airworthy, taking care of his busy elderly parents that live in the middle of everything going on, and did I mention that he also farms? So the short of it for me is that he is pretty burnt out after the season is over, even though he meant well, it didn't take much of a reason for him to take the day off, like taking kids to the dentist or parents to town, an appointment with an accountant, etc. He really didn't care to work in too much wind and would quit much sooner than I. Later the same week that Bob had burnt off my ears for turning off the gas, we were still flying out of his runway. I had completed four or five loads that morning and noticed Bob wasn't flying again. Still under stress from not being able to keep up with all the work coming in, I got out of the plane and found Bob by his shop and proceeded to fly off the handle. "What the hell? You should be flying. You are always making up reasons not to fly!" Then Bob calmly answered me, "Tim, a cylinder is blown off the airplane." After I calmed down, Bob talked me into using Jerry Abbott to fix the engine. I normally would repair the blown engine cylinders myself, mostly to save money. Bob convinced me that I could get a lot more work done while someone else fixed it, and he was probably right, but I think he just felt more comfortable flying behind Jerry's work. Who knows, maybe he's right.

Later that week, I took off from Bob's, and I had just passed over some woods en route to a field and was now over open farmland that had a high-tension power line passing through it about half mile in front of me. Suddenly a loud bam came from the center of the propeller. Whatever broke, broke so hard; I saw a little puff of smoke. The prop and engine were violently shaking. Immediately I remembered what the guy told me in Batesville when I was trying to bend my prop back with the pliers, that it would shake off the front of the plane before you could turn it off. I looked at the power lines with a runway only a quarter mile beyond them, and I thought, "Over or under?" Then I thought, "One thing for sure it will go under," and instantly I pulled power with my left hand and jammed the stick forward with my right. Luck was with me; I flared out under the power lines at only about a fifteen-degree angle to the soybeans and stopped two feet short of a ten-foot-deep ditch. I hadn't gotten a scratch on me or the plane. This was in the days before I started keeping a cell phone in the plane, so I had to walk back to Bob's, going through several big ditches all filled with stickers. By the time I got back, I was bleeding with all the cuts and scratches from the briars and stickers. They thought I had been in a wreck. We waited until dark, and then Bob pulled the plane to that runway on the other side of the power line with his tractor.

That night, when we got home, the farmer I was spreading cover crop for, who also owned the field I landed in, called me, "I heard you landed in my field. How many beans did you tear up?" I answered, "Hardly any. I landed right with the rows," and he hung up without another word. That guy didn't care if I broke my neck or totaled my plane, but he was going to make me pay for the beans!

Sometime later, I stopped in to see a friendly competitor. Skip was having a rough day pleasing the customers. He said, "You know if I was spraying for a farmer and I crashed and burned right in the middle of his field," now pointing at me as he continued on, "I believe that farmer without hesitation would call you and ask if you can see all that smoke from the burning plane? Can you just start there and spray the rest of the field? Never even calling 911 for me!" I think I knew exactly how he felt.

The next spring, this same farmer wanted me to spray some wheat. He complained that nobody ever sprays this one corner where the road turns, and the power lines cross at a funny angle. So, when I sprayed that field, I tried to run under the low wires. I got a little too low; the wheels hit deep in the wheat, and the prop was chopping the wheat to bits. I could feel the wheat sucking the plane in, so I pulled back as hard as I could, and slowly the plane came up out of the wheat. The wheat did break two of the plastic blades on my pump, but I managed not to nose over. A day or so later, the farmer asked what happened to his wheat? I didn't want to pay for the wheat, so I told him that I saw some teenagers parking there.

GOOD ole Bob, he gave me another one of his big tips. I should have learned by now to take those hot tips with a grain of salt, but I am a slow learner. I got a call from some guy named Nate wanting a plane ferried home from near Branson, and he said Bob had recommended me. It was the dead of winter, and I could use the money. Nate had bought this experimental home-built plane that was supposed to resemble a P-51 Mustang. Nate didn't have a license and hadn't even taken his first lesson. I agreed for a thousand dollars and expenses. I also told him to buy round-trip tickets, they were normally cheaper than one-way, and who knows about the plane's condition or the weather. Nate agreed to carry me to BWI, gave me the tickets with the thousand, and dropped me off at the terminal. When checking in, I noticed the tickets were only one-way. Arriving at Springfield, as the airliner taxied in, I saw sitting off to the side about twenty De Havilland Dash 8 commuter planes, all in various stages of disassemble. I thought "It looks like the end of the line again."

In the terminal, a guy was holding a cardboard sign with my name on it. He looked me up and down, and the first thing that he said, "Oh my, I told him to send someone small," before he even said hi. Don, the seller, lived about 40 miles away in a flying community, and the plane was kept across the runway at his buddy's home/hangar. Don told Nate that he would include a new battery and spark plugs, and after it wouldn't start, Don decided to live up to the deal, at least halfway. We rode into town and bought a battery. After it did start, it ran like crap, so I cleaned all the old plugs, drained the car gas, put new gas in, then it ran halfway good.

The small plane had a cockpit that should have been a single seat; instead, it had two narrow seats with a small console in the middle. Between the seats was a plywood disk on edge, with a red mark; this was attached to the landing gear and would spin as the gear went up and down. The red mark indicated if the gear was in the proper position. The whole thing was driven by a 12-volt DEWALT drill, held in place by two big hose clamps. The handle had been sawed off so that the wires could be attached. The wires made their way halfway up the control stick and ended with a toggle switch, which you just pushed up or down. There were no gear lock lights, just that red mark. Later, I found that I had to grab the plywood disk and help spin it, and sometimes I would have to work the gear a little up and down before it would take off spinning. The plane itself was built out of wood and covered with fiberglass and had a sliding canopy. The tailwheel must have come off a shopping cart. The engine had come from a ground power unit and converted for an airplane. The woodwork, what I could see, looked to be skillfully done, the fiberglass was so so, and the steel framework not so good. The welding that was holding things together, such as the frame, brackets, engine mounts, and other parts, looked like lumps of bubble gum. Very few of the bolts that held the rest together were long enough, but in most cases, the bolts were too short, and the end was recessed in one or two threads of the nut, and not sticking out two or three threads as required. If you stood back maybe fifty feet or so, it didn't look bad, painted up in blue and silver with D-Day markings and Crazy Horse painted on the cowing. I have seen the P-51 Mustang Crazy Horse in different flying magazines. It did, in fact, resemble it, but mostly just in paint.

By the time the thing was ready to roll, it was late enough that I decided to just shoot a few landings, takeoffs, and fly around a little while to be sure that the plane was okay, then get a good night's sleep and go home in the morning.

As I squirmed and shimmied my way in, Don climbed on the wing and showed me a few different things. Before jumping down, he demonstrated the elevator trim knob on the left side panel by sliding it back and forth. With that, I lined up at the end of the narrow grass runway and gave it the gas. The faster it went, the more right rudder was needed to stay straight. Some right rudder is normal, but I had my foot buried in it and it wasn't enough. I had a hard time keeping in the middle of the runway. By this time, I was about three quarters down the runway up on the main gear. I felt the stick, and it was still heavy. I was now nearing the end of the runway and looking at some uncut corn ahead, but the thing was still not lifting off. I gave the stick a firm nudge back, and with that, the thing went straight up. At that steep angle, with the wheels still down, it was running out of speed fast, I pushed hard forward on the stick, and the nose just wouldn't go over. "Oh shit, it looks like I'll be coming down ass first," is what I was thinking. Then I slid the trim forward, and the nose went over. On my "oh shit" scale, it was only a one but still got my attention. Evidently, the trim tab was built too big in relation to the elevators. It was impossible to easily overpower the trim with the stick, like it was supposed to. Luckily, I had experience with flying banner planes where no one bothered to set the trim, you just cranked it after taking off, so my left hand automatically went for the trim without hesitation. After shaking out the plane some, I came in to land, already preparing for the left pull. Still, it seemed to pull even more, so I wanted to tap the right brake just to keep going straight. My right foot was already buried on the floorboard. The thing had heel brakes, but whoever built this piece of crap, put the pedal inside and halfway up of the rudder pedal. I dared not take my foot off the rudder to hit the brake, at the last second, I was able to get my left foot on the right brake; it doesn't sound too hard until I remind you that the plane is so small, that even a five-year-old would have a hard time fitting his feet in there. After maintaining some control rolling out, I thought I'll do another takeoff and landing, thinking that I had this thing licked. Gave it the gas, once again fighting the right rudder, and this time just missing one of the left runway lights, only because I broke ground first. After a couple more takeoffs and landings, I taxied over to Don's pad and parked.

As I got out, he said, "You broke it!" Pointing under the thing (the "thing" doesn't deserve to be called a plane) the left wheel was tilting at a pretty good angle. We discovered that the bottom two nuts holding the spindle flange on were missing. I turned the top two nuts off with my fingers; the only reason they didn't come off is that the top is under compression load (not pulling on it). The reason was that most of the bolts in this "thing" were not long enough. Normal practice for aircraft is to use nuts with cotter pins or use stop nuts with nylon inserts, to prevent the nuts from becoming loose. Because this plane used mostly stop nuts, it was essential to have the bolt's threads come out beyond the nut so the nylon would work. We needed longer bolts to fix this, but someone had welded a piece of steel to stiffen the gear leg over the short bolts that we needed to replace. So, the bolts just spun, and there was no way to get a wrench on it. We had it fixed up after borrowing a grinder from the guy across the runway and a trip to Ace Hardware.

While talking to the guy with the grinder, I found out that Nate had driven all the way out here with a rollback truck when he bought the plane. But the way the plane was constructed, there wasn't a way to disassemble it to fit on the truck. The grinder guy had a plane that looked much like this one, so then Nate offered him fifteen hundred to fly it to Salisbury, Maryland, but the grinder guy wouldn't fly it, knowing about the plane. Don was an older guy with lots of experience and had flown Night Hawks and Black Widows in World War II, and now did some aircraft buying, selling, and trading. He drove me to the motel, and on the way, I think he was starting to feel a little guilty. He told me to tell Nate that he would let him have a Cessna 150 instead of the mini-Mustang even up for what he had already paid. After what I had just seen, that was a great idea. In my room, I called Nate and told him. Since Nate hadn't even flown, the Cessna would be an excellent trainer. I emphasized what a piece of junk the mini-Mustang was, and I told him that I had over ten thousand hours in taildraggers, but that "thing" almost kicked my butt, and that "thing" would probably kill him and his instructor. But he would have no part of it. He wanted the mini-Mustang and that's all it was to it.

Sitting there with no ticket home and feeling short-changed by five hundred bucks, I rationalized that I had just made four landings and takeoffs and only needed three to get home. So, I would fly it home, but would not fly it to another airstrip where he was to rent a hangar later that month, as I said I would. In fact, I thought if I get close enough to home for my wife to come get me, that's where I'm leaving it. Reading the logbooks later that night, the builder had entries like: (Reshaped right-wing still flies left-wing heavy, moved engine forward eleven inches still not right, modified the tail was going to test fly but too windy I'll try again tomorrow). On top of that gibberish, the hours didn't make sense. I was told that it had four hundred plus hours, but I could only see about thirty. I also noticed that Don, with tons of experience, only ever flew it once when he first bought it four years ago (no wonder), even though the logbook had a signed off inspection every year. I would sure like to meet that blind SOB inspector that signed it off.

The next morning, I took off for home, feeling a little apprehensive about the plane. Instead of going directly due east as I normally would, where there was nothing but the Ozarks, hills, rocks, and trees under me for hundreds of miles with nowhere to safely land if the plane had a problem, I flew south for about a hundred miles. Then I'd go east with a pretty good number of small airports in the line of flight most of the way home. Don had explained the wing tanks didn't need flushing like we had done the main tank because they had been drained. The wing tanks pumped into the main tank right ahead of the windshield. That tank gravity-fed the engine. About forty-five minutes after leaving Don, still over the Ozarks, I hit the switch to pump fuel from the wing tanks into the main tank. Then I quickly turned it back off, thinking you dummy, everything is going well and don't change a thing until getting in the clear. It needed half-right rudder to keep the plane straight and level, and the stick was against my right leg, which was pinned against the console, making my leg numb. Nonetheless, I made the next stop okay, and even managed to tame that left pull on landing. Having made it that far without trouble and filling up with avgas instead of autogas, it looked as if things were going to be alright. I'd plan to stop just short of Nashville. As I approached that stop, I had plenty of fuel and another hour of daylight, so I punched in the GPS another airport about seventy miles ahead.

As I pressed on, circumnavigating around the Nashville air space, I hit the switch to transfer fuel from the wing tanks to the main tank. It was only about a minute until the engine started to sputter. I glanced at my GPS and noticed an airport ahead and to the right in about 10 miles. I immediately turned towards it, then I pulled the carburetor heat; as I pulled it, the engine came back to life. But as I pulled it all the way out, the engine lost power, so I pushed it in halfway, and once again, the engine came back to life. Feeling relieved, I started to turn back to my original heading, but that was short-lived; within less than a minute, the engine went back to sputtering, only making five or six hundred rpm. At fifty-five hundred feet, it looked probable that I might make that airport on the GPS. However, I was on a tight budget when I bought the GPS, so it had a small screen which was zoomed out 50 miles. Since I was not terribly profi-cient with the settings on the GPS, I decided it was best to leave it alone rather than lose the whole picture, making it difficult to find the airport. As I was passing through fifteen hundred feet, I still hadn't located the runway. Now I was looking around for plan B, still on the outskirts of Nashville. All I could see were buildings like stores, malls, and warehouses. What roads and parking lots there were, were full of cars, one main highway full of traffic, and no rivers or water in sight. So, I got ready to head for the train tracks, thinking is it best with gear up or down? About the time I really had to make a commitment, I made out the runway dead ahead. I was perpendicular to it and lined up with the middle with no chance of getting to either end. I was too low to do anything but go straight in, but high enough that I could land too deep, so I simultaneously put down the gear and dove at what looked to be an 84 Lumber roof, rounding out just feet above the building, hoping to bleed off speed before the airport. The plane had no flaps or spoilers, so the speed didn't bleed off as much as I hoped. I touched down as soon as I crossed the fence and made sure to stick the wheels, hoping that the drag of the small wheels in the grass would help slow things down. The plane was still rolling out fast and I didn't want to try brakes at that speed, risking nosing over or skidding out. I had landed on the grass, but now running out of grass I shot across the taxiway, then back on to the grass between the runway and taxiway, in the process taking out a taxiway light, next shooting across the runway, and back into the rough grass and heading for a ravine full of rocks; and if I made it through that, a fence ahead. At this point, I have to admit I was really running out of plans, but just then the right gear collapsed and the plane turned sideways with the left wing towards the rocks, still sliding pretty fast. I grasped the framework above my head and prepared for the plane to start cartwheeling, knowing that the main fuel tank was just about in my lap, with a plane that was made of wood. All I could see in my mind was the James Bond movies where the cars and planes explode, and most of them seem to blow up even before impact, thinking this is going to really suck! But then, the other gear collapsed, and the plane slid to a stop just as smooth as sitting on a living room couch! Still, it was a #2 on the oh shit scale.

Standing next to the plane after all the dust settled, scratching my head wondering what's next, a man walked out to me, handed me his cell phone, and said, "This guy wants to talk to you." The man from the FAA wanted to know what happened and then asked what ratings I had. He explained that if the damage was bad enough, it would be classified as an accident, and a written report would have to be made. But the damage was light, it would just be an incident, and no report was necessary. Then he said that since I was an IA (inspector), I could make the decision. I explained that I may be partial in this situation but believed it really was very minor. Lucky it was late Friday afternoon, and I don't think the FAA man wanted to ruin his weekend, so he agreed. Next, I had found a tow truck to move the plane to the ramp. I put it way in the back near the fence, far away from everything, pulled the wheels down, and set it on them, so it looked just like any other plane. On examination, the only thing wrong with the gear was what looked to be a piece of soft metal 3/8 inch all thread that made things go up and down, probably from Ace Hardware, was bent up like a pretzel. The composite blades were busted off the prop. I went to that same 84 Lumber, bought a 2x4 and a couple of ratchet straps, and tied the gear legs apart. Gave the office Nate's number along with mine, rented a car, and went home.

This should be the end of this story, but like the gift that just keeps on giving, I received a call some three months later that the airport wanted something done with the plane. Once again, I explained that it was Nate's plane, and I had nothing to do with it from here on out. I started getting letters billing me for storage. Then they started sending legal letters, each one more threatening, and unreal storage charges like fifty dollars a day. I would find out that Nate never would answer them or acknowledge the plane, fearing he would get in trouble with the FAA. I had told this story to a couple hangar rats at the Salisbury airport. They took an interest, and Nate agreed to just sign over the plane for no cost, still fearing some kind of retribution from FAA for a plane that didn't meet codes or for the emergency landing. So some of my favorite hangar rats, Kenny, Mike, and Charley borrowed my trailer to go get the plane. Facing thousands of dollars the airport wanted for storage, Mike put on a nice pair of slacks, dress shirt, and tie, and apparently, the airport office was led to believe that he was with the FAA Airport Appropriations Department that would make the decisions on how much money the airport would receive next year. The office saw fit to adjust the storage amount to the twenty-five dollars the sign on the wall said for monthly tiedowns, so now they paid just a couple hundred dollars. Facing the same problem Nate did, the plane wouldn't come apart in such a manner to fit on the trailer. They then went to that same 84 Lumber store and bought a cordless saw and cut the wings off about a couple feet out from the fuselage, cutting right through the tanks, spar, and all, then loaded it up and brought it home. The gift just keeps on giving. After they returned the trailer I fixed the bent hitch and replaced the broken lights and never said a word.

One day while over at the Salisbury airport, I stopped by Kenny's hangar, and out of curiosity, I checked the gascolator. Surprisingly it appeared to be pretty clean and dry. Then as I took a fingernail and pulled down the screen, gas ran out. Strange. Looking at the screen, it looked clear until I noticed one of the little squares that I had touched with my fingernail really was clear, and the rest were shellacked over. The best we can tell is that the film that autogas leaves on the walls of gas tanks will loosen after a couple hours with the stronger avgas and go through the fuel system clogging up the screen. After a while, the guys gave up and lost interest, and it was sold on eBay. I got a call from a gentleman who sounded very excited. "I heard you flew this plane, what do you think?" He told me he had sixty hours in a Piper Cherokee 140. I explained how many hours I had, and my experience with that plane, what a piece of crap the plane was, and told him that it would probably kill him. Sounded as if he might cry when he hung up.

THAT next summer, I was spraying along a poplar route to the beach not far from Bob's runway. The way the field was shaped, it had me spraying towards and away from the road, moving over fifty feet each pass, when I noticed a car pulled alongside the road; the car would jockey forward then backward, trying to line up with my next pass. Couldn't believe my eyes; the car could have doubled for Chevy Chase's monster station wagon on its way to Wally World, baggage strapped on the roof and all. The husband got out of the car, walked out in the field, lined up with my pass, and took my picture. This meant that I had to cut off the spray, and pull up early to come back later to spray the missed area. The next pass, the same thing happened, and then the following pass, he moved over in my flight path again. So, this time, I turned off the spray early again but held the plane down, then pulling up just enough to go over the man, almost giving him a haircut, then back down and under the wires, and made like I was flying away. After the station wagon left, I returned and finished the job and flew home.

Not long after I was home, the phone rang. It was Ralph, Bob's nephew. "What did you do?" I could hear some man yelling at Bob in the background. "Don't tell me that wasn't you, I know it was that plane." Ralph went on to explain that the man with his family in the Chevy Chase wagon was just giving Uncle Robert holy hell. He wouldn't believe Bob that he wasn't the man spraying, as he was pointing at Bob's Ag Cat, "I'd know that plane anywhere! Don't tell me it wasn't you!" I must admit, after all the hot tips that turned sour, like the mini-Mustang or filling my father-in-law's car with dust, and all the other predicaments Bob put me in, it felt good to put one on him.

FOR years, as the season drew to a close, Bob and I would say that as soon as the work is over, we're going fishing and just relax. Anybody that is in our business will know what I mean. We pack a whole year's worth of work into just a few summer months, and we work from four in the morning until well after dark, seven days a week, with no breaks. But for years, it never happened. We could never get our schedules to jive. Normally, Bob had to take the kids to the dentist or parents to the doctors.

One Sunday after the season was over, after all the pilots had gone home and the customers were squared away, I pulled out my boat, which I bought new before I started in the crop dusting business. It had only been in the water twice since I bought it twelve years earlier. I bought it on a momentary impulse and just had to have it that day for a family get-together at our beach place. I couldn't remember what deal I made, but Kay made the payment every month. After five years, Kay informed me that she had just ripped the last payment out of the book and sent it off. I said "good," since we don't use it anyway. A few weeks later, a new payment book came in the mail for five more years. So, I pulled it out with my new pickup (the first new pickup I ever bought, I had always bought used ones before) and vowed to take extra special care of it. I parked the truck and boat on the hangar pad to wash it and install the third new battery in this boat with a total time of nine hours.

The next morning, I made up my mind that even if I had to handcuff Bob, we were going fishing! As I was sitting on the couch putting on my shoes, the farmer that tends my farm knocked on the door. "Have you been out back lately? you got one hell of a mess!" I could see right from the doorway something was wrong. I rushed back behind the hangar and saw that the irrigation system that is supposed to quit at the corner of the old chicken house at the stop had kept going, wrapping around the building. The bent up system continued moving, swooping up an Ag Cat parked by the windsock, dragging it backwards two hundred feet, all the time ripping the heck out of the top wing. Finally, the plane-embedded irrigation pushed the plane up and over the front of the new pickup, crushing the cab, where it came to rest. Then the irrigation ran into the hangar, smashing the corner of the building. Unbelievably, the irrigation tire was still turning on the cement pad, leaving a pile of rubber 4 inches tall.

Just to throw this in, Kay had loaned our Honda car to our grandson Kris against my advice. He totaled it the day before, so this meant I was out one car, one truck, one plane, one irrigation, and a damaged building in 24 hours. Worst of all, the boat was trapped behind this mess, and we couldn't go fishing!

P.S. About ten years later I got that boat out and removed that new battery that had never been used (it had gone bad and traded it for a new battery) then something came up; I still haven't used the boat as of this writing. And that truck that I had taken special care of it has been damaged by trailers twice, had the roof caved in, and not once but two different times trees have dropped on it. It is a Dodge, and my friends call it Christine named after the car in Stephen King's movie.

Chapter 13
Some Of The Folks I've Met

Early springtime my third year, Dave called me up and asked if I would be interested in riding to North Carolina, spending the night, and then flying on to Georgia with him and Craig to pick up two planes. I answered, "Sure, why not?" The first night we arrived in North Carolina about nine o'clock and stayed in his large fifth wheel camper. We had only been there for few minutes when Dave picked up the phone and called some young lady to come over, but then he turned to me and asked if I wanted this lady to bring a friend for me. I just turned to Dave and said, "You know I fight the weather every day, I'm always fighting with mechanical problems, money is always a problem, and keeping the farmers happy is a hell of a job. All of the surrounding homeowners complain, and I think all of the regulators hate me. The only thing really working out for me is my marriage, and you want me to screw that up?" After fifteen minutes an attractive blond lady showed up, and she and Dave went into his room. I slept in the back bedroom at the opposite end, or you might say tried to sleep, with all the rocking the trailer was doing.

The next morning after Dave called the shop in Georgia, they said it would take another day before the planes were ready. The plan had been to meet up with Craig, Dave's partner and fly down to Georgia in Craig's V-tail Bonanza to pick up Craig's and Dave's turbine Thrushes. With the day to kill, we decided to get our medicals. Craig knew of a doctor located on the sound of the inland side to the Outer Banks. We boarded Craig's V-tail and landed in the middle of nowhere, not a tree or building in sight, on an airstrip used for fire operations, but it didn't look used recently. Craig called a number and someone came and picked us up and carried us to a small fishing town. The doctor's office was in a nondescript cinder block building. Everything, including the furniture, was kinda old and looked as it came from the Andy Griffin show. The eighty-five-year-old doctor and the nurse, his equivalent-aged wife, were happy to see us but also perturbed that we hadn't buzzed the office. Their system was, you buzz the office, and then they come to pick you up.

The nurse was very pleasant but unsteady on her feet; twice I caught her from falling as she was maneuvering between the countertop with all the instruments and the area around the examining table. I could hear Dave struggling with the eye chart in the next room. "Ah, Q, M, R, C, U," then a long pause, then, "G." Then the doctor said, "Doesn't that look more like a C." Dave's reply, "Yeah, that's what I meant, C." Somehow, with the doc's help, he managed to ace all three lines! Next, it was Craig's turn to look at the colored numbers surrounded by all the colored spots. Craig couldn't make them out, so the doctor opened a book with one whole page painted blue and asked what color it was, then flipped to one that the whole page was painted bright red and asked, "what color is this?" Then said, "Good, that's all we need to know."

The next day, with fresh medicals in hand, we flew to Americus, Georgia. Dave's plane wasn't quite ready, and Craig's wouldn't be done until the next day. Killing time, I toured an overgrown field next to the airport full of aging ag planes, some with no wings, some looked to be complete, but neglected with weeds growing all around and over them, there were about twenty planes all in neat rows. I was told that they were brought here from Czechoslovakia as an alternative ag plane, but they couldn't get them certified. They appeared to be well built, probably too heavy to carry any kind of payload, but it struck me funny that there were school bus fans mounted over the panel to keep the pilot cool.

By the afternoon Dave's plane was ready, I was to follow in Craig's V-tail back to North Carolina, and Craig was to bring his plane home the next day. Craig gave me a quick rundown about his plane. He told me that the parking brake handle seems backward to him in the way it operates. Dave took off first, and when I taxied in position, I quickly tried the parking brake each way. I couldn't tell any differences, so I left it at what I thought was off. The plane seemed slow to build speed, so I abandoned the takeoff and put the brake in the opposite direction and proceeded to taxi back. Craig called me on the radio and asked, "What's wrong?" I explained that I thought I had the brake wrong and took off without any further ado. When we stopped for fuel, Dave checked in with Craig about our progress. After he hung up, he told me that he wasn't supposed to tell me, but Craig said that my brake deal made him nervous, so he went and had his airplane insurance doubled right after I left.

When we arrived in North Carolina, it was just about dark. I landed first and had to talk Dave into landing there because his ag plane didn't have good landing lights, and the runway wasn't lighted. Before he would land he had me check for deer's known to be on the runway.

OVER the years, I've had many guys admire the way that crop dusters fly and say they would also like to do that. Out of all these crop dusters wannabes, only my friend Wes has ever followed through with getting a pilot's license and then went ahead to get a tailwheel endorsement. Shortly after Wes got his license, I had bought another Ag Cat. Wes agreed to fly me down to Mississippi and then follow me back. It would help him build cross-country time. Wes borrowed his friend's Piper 140 and flew over to pick me up. We were ready to leave with the plane packed full of luggage, food, drinks, tools, GPS, and a radio to install in the Ag Cat. Wes is a big guy, over six feet tall and I'm guessing over three hundred pounds, and since he would be the pilot he got in first. I climbed in next, and I am not small either. We taxied out with full tanks of gas and took off to the south toward the trees into the wind. That poor little Piper had all that it could handle and more! After breaking ground, Wes veered a little to the left because the trees were slightly lower. I don't think you could have gotten a sheet of paper between the plane and the trees. The headwind was more off to the right, so we should have turned a little right to get the plane into the wind, but Wes turned left. I don't blame him, because there were many trees to the right, and the plane just wallowed, not climbing at all. Off to the left was a clearing, then Bennett Airport, but when Wes turned left, it gave a bit of tailwind. We sunk all the way down to about five feet off the ground before we started to fly again; I believe we were another state away before we were able to climb to a thousand feet.

Somewhere over the Carolinas, I had gotten comfortable enough to doze off when suddenly things went quiet. I thought the engine had failed. Talk about waking up in a hurry! It turns out Wes had gotten a little befuddled on his navigation and that one of his instructors taught him to cut the power back to buy more time. After I got my heart restarted, I told him that I might have to shoot him if he ever did that again.

Somewhere over South Carolina, we passed a radio tower thirty-two hundred feet tall. I'd been relaxing, feeling fairly secure as long as Wes didn't touch the throttle, but seeing that tower at eye level, somehow, I lost that secure feeling.

That night we stayed in Rome, Georgia. We met up with two doctors flying a Cirrus loaded with all the bells and whistles, en route to some kind of Cirrus event in Florida. We all went out to a steak house for dinner and a few drinks, the comradery of meeting up with other pilots traveling was great. One doctor was telling us that his specialty was operating on hemorrhoids and explained exactly how the procedure is done while I was trying to eat my steak dinner, a couple of beers helped me get through it.

The next day somewhere over Alabama, air traffic control called us and advised Wes to deviate to the south fifteen miles to avoid a thunderstorm. Wes looked out all the windows and radioed back that it looked fine to him and he wanted to just keep going straight. The controller called back and said in a stern voice, "Whatever you wish." In just a few minutes, Wes had flown directly into a pretty mean thunderstorm and was, to say, a little uptight, in fact, a whole lot uptight. I told him don't even think about touching that throttle. I saw a hole in the storm off to the left and told Wes to head for that. Then Wes called the controller and asked for help, and they handed him off with a change of frequency three times in the next five minutes. I am pretty sure those controllers were sitting across from each other, getting even for not taking their advice. Things got a little rough and it seemed like the hole closed up on us, but eventually we broke out. Once in the clear, Wes wanted to make a stop to regain his composure. I couldn't talk him out of it. Wes looked on the chart, saw a county airport nearby, and asked the controller to vector him to it. Once we found the airport and were getting ready to line up on it, we notice big Xs on each end of the runways and you could see trees growing out of the holes in the roofs of the buildings. It was obvious that this airport had not been used for many years. Once again, the controller didn't tell us that; I suppose he was still holding a grudge for Wes not listening to him. Somewhere over the beginning of Mississippi, we landed at another county airport, only to find that it had just been sold to a flying community and had no gas. However, it worked out for us since we sat out a passing thunderstorm before continuing on. Now we were sweating about low fuel, but we made Oxford college (Ole Miss), got fuel, and went on without further ado.

The next morning we picked up the plane and flew it to Batesville where I had met Dennis and Jim many years earlier while stuck there with a bent prop when I brought home my first plane. I wanted to thank them again for all the help back then and show them that I had learned to fly. While I was there, I fixed the backward trim tab that didn't move enough either.

I noticed a drip at the bottom of the carburetor but thought it would be okay to get home.

At the next fuel stop, Wes complained that he had to fly with flaps, and couldn't I go any faster; I assured him the Ag Cat was doing all it could. The gas was now a pretty fast drip under the carburetor, so I borrowed a cake of soap and rubbed it on the bottom of the carburetor, and the drip stopped. The next stop was a bust, nobody around to give us fuel, just a note on the door with a phone number that nobody answered, so we pressed on to the next nearest airport. It turns out we were in Muscle Shoals, which I had heard about, and is mentioned in the song Sweet Home Alabama. We spent the night there; I only wish I had had more time to look around. Once again, I noticed that drip was more like a small stream when gassing up, so I rubbed more soap on it. It appeared the soap was working, kinda.

At each stop, the leak was getting worse. It looked like I would need a lot more soap, but we kept pressing on. Thank God we made Accomack on the Eastern Shore at about 7 pm. It was now an hour from home, and the weather was coming in fast. We fueled up and I used the last of the soap and rushed to beat the thunderstorms. I took off first as the sky turned black. There was a tunnel of light towards the Bay, and I headed for it. I looked back in time to see Wes starting his takeoff roll when two bolts of lightning struck, one on each side of his plane. He chopped the power and taxied back to the parking. After quite a bit of coaching over the radio, I talked him into trying again and assured him that it was okay over the Bay where I was. We had to land at Laurel since I don't have runway lights, and now it was getting dark. My gas leak must have gotten worst because when I landed at Laurel, I ran out of gas and had only flown one hour. I figure I lost about thirty gallons. The next day I stopped at Lowe's and bought a screw that had a rubber washer on it, used for attaching metal roofing, and screwed that in the hole in the bottom of the carburetor. It worked like a charm! Poured in a couple five-gallon cans of gas and made it home.

About a month later, Wes asked if he could sit in one of the Ag Cats. He could barely fit, and there was no way he would have been able to fly it. And just like that, he gave up on his dream of being a crop duster after working towards it for two years. I told him they make more roomy planes, but he just lost interest. He is probably better off, for he hasn't ruined his flying hobby, and he makes good money selling slush machines up and down the East Coast. I asked where does he sell these slush machines? Maybe at all the 7-Eleven stores? He told me those are called slush machines, but his is the machine to place a heart in when it is out of the body during a transplant.

CAN'T remember exactly when I met Ron, but what a character! One of the first things I remember was overhearing him trying to convince Dave that he had just done him a big favor by wrecking the plane that Dave had loaned him, because Dave stood to gain from the insurance. Ron's father had been a successful duster in North Carolina back in the hay day. I once saw a picture of his father's operation with at least six Stearman duster planes lined up with the same paint job and successive tail numbers. You could tell by the picture that guy really had it going on. I heard that Ron once had some of the biggest farmers around, and he was a gifted pilot.

One of the things that Ron loved to do was to find alternative methods of making things work, which I'm not sure on an airplane is a good thing. Some of his cost-saving inventions were almost genius and a little scary. He showed me that a wheel barrel tire would fit on the tailwheel and only cost about ten bucks. I complimented him on it even though the writing on the tire said not to exceed 15 mph. I am unsure whether he was taking all these cost-saving initiatives because of the declining business, or some of these alternative methods were leading to business declining.

Somewhere around 2005, Kay and I went down to visit Dave and check out his new house and runway in North Carolina. That night we went into town to a dance club to hear "Carolina beach music." This music was all the old soul-rock from the late 50s early 60s being revived by the young folks. That night, The Chairman of The Board was playing. The young guys and girls were singing along with these old songs. Kay asked one of them how they knew the songs and they answered that they had dug out their parents' and grandparents' old records. Ron was there looking like a million bucks wearing nice khaki pants, dock siders, a dark blue blazer with a Pratt and Whitney logo, and wearing a gold chain. Ron is over six feet tall, medium build, with just enough gray hair mixed in to look really distinguished. This guy just had it going on! I believe if he told you that he was a Ferrari salesman, you'd believe it. He really was in true form that night, dancing with all the women; even now, when I think of him, that's the image I see.

A couple of years later, I took a Cessna Ag Truck down to Dave's as a favor, and I picked up the plane in Felton Delaware. John had been flying it recently and told me not to worry about the right fuel tank. It'll eventually pick it up. I stopped at Salisbury, topped off the gas, and headed down the coast to North

Carolina. As I approached the Bay Bridge-Tunnel, I noticed that the right tank read full, and I'm sure it was right because gas was still trailing out the gas cap. Meanwhile, the left gauge was about a quarter. Now I had to circumnavigate over the ocean to get around the Oceana military base, which I did in a slip the whole way with the right wing raised, hoping gas would start feeding out of the right tank. With gas seeping out of the right gas cap and the left gauge on empty, I reached a small airport towards the Outer Banks and landed for fuel. If I would have had to do a go-around, I am sure it would have sucked that tank dry. Nobody was around. It was like a ghost town, but luckily it had a credit card gas pump. The right tank took none and the left took all but a gallon less than its size.

When I arrived at Dave's, Ron was standing there to greet me; in fact, he was blocking me from climbing off the wing, saying "Being as you are down here, I thought I'd run you over to my place so you could annual inspect my planes." I did manage to get a word in edgewise to the Cessna's new owner and advised him to check that right tank; later, he told me that a mud dobbler had clogged the vent pipe. With that said, Ron whisked me off to God knows where, twisting and turning on all the back roads until we arrived at his place. There sat two beat-up looking Ag Cats and a Weatherly that had one landing gear strut coming out of the bottom of one wing and spring landing gear mounted on the other side but was painted up orange with stars and bars to look like the General Lee on the *Dukes of Hazard*. The plane was named General Lee.

The first Ag Cat had been fixed up for Ron's new ag flight school. He had removed the chemical tank, installed a front seat, which was a lawn chair held in place by plastic wire ties, and the windshield came from an Air Tractor, which sorta fit. He didn't want the students to get befuddled with extra controls, so the mixture knob was disconnected. The prop had been disabled with hose clamps on the counterweights. He needed a belly tank to hold spray, so he had split a tank from a hot water heater down the middle and welded a flat metal plate on the half tank, being sure to let it hang past the tank about two feet, which he mounted the chemical pump on. All this was mounted up under the plane. The plane had some kinda wavy black poly hose, probably what is made to bury for lawn irrigation mounted in place of the spray bars. Once again, Ron was proud to find a more cost-effective and readily available alternative. He had replaced the fabric tail feathers with sheets of clear Plexiglas that had about a million holes drilled around the perimeter and wire ties holding them on. He must have used a truckload of plastic wire ties on this plane. I'm thinking this could make AN bolts obsolete. He showed me how if you use contact paper that you can get at any Kmart and stick it on the inside of the Plexiglas, it has the appearance of a base coat clear coat paint job. Plywood was used for wing extensions, and there was no electrical system, so the Pratt & Whitney 450 had to be hand propped. All of the planes had wheelbarrow tires.

Oh my God, if I sign off on any of this, putting my name in one of these logbooks, if he even has books, I surely will lose my license and go to jail! What do I do? After a couple minutes, I told Ron it's getting dark, and I will need to spend more time tomorrow going over this. So, he took me back to Dave's. On the way back, I couldn't help thinking, Ron has been down here many years doing all these unorthodox things, and much more I've heard, how come the FAA hasn't bothered him? Then

I thought, I'll bet there is a couple of older gray-haired FAA men getting ready to retire, arguing over who's going to deal with Ron. I imagine the conversation, "I'm not going to inspect him, I would have to write reports the rest of my life."

"Well, I'm not getting caught up in it either; let's just wait until we get a new guy."

I told Dave my dilemma, and he said no problem, we will just get up early and head back to Delaware. The next morning the bedroom door flung open at 5:30. "Come on Tim Curry, we have a lot to do!" Ron somehow had let himself in. I just put the pillow over my head and thought this nightmare would never end. Luckily, Dave to the rescue; he told Ron that he had a family emergency and we had to go right away.

Some years later, when I needed Ag Cat parts, Ron said he had some parts he would sell me. Kris, my grandson, agreed to go with me, so off we went in a pickup truck pulling a trailer. We stopped by Dave's and he gave us directions and told us that the phones don't work in that part of the country. We were having a hard time finding Ron's place. At one point, trapped on a dead-end dirt road and frustrated, I slammed the truck in reverse, turned sharply, totally forgetting about the trailer, and jackknifed it into the truck. At this point the backside of my truck was caved in and the tire was hissing air out the hole the trailer put in it. And we had no phone service. We made a run for the 7-Eleven we passed ten miles ago, flying down all these dirt roads and pulling in the parking lot just as the tire went flat.

Changing the tire: what a nightmare, by the way, did you know? The factory puts a different kind of locking lug nut on each wheel, and you need a special adapter. Only after we tried vise grips, a pipe wrench and everything else, did we find that special adapter hidden under the back seat. I know this now! Finally, about twenty miles down mostly dirt roads, we found the heavy logging equipment junkyard that Ron now lived in. As we looked around, there was no signs of life. Out of the empty shop in the middle of the place, we followed an orange extension cord for quite a ways as it zigzagged around old broken-down pieces of equipment. It led to an old Winnebago with no wheels that sat lopsided held up by various rusty pieces and parts. We banged on the door and out came Ron. The change of fortune hadn't slowed him down at all; he loaded us up in a Blazer that said something about the logging company on the tag, but he said it was his. He showed us around the area, pointing to different farms he claimed to own or had owned, telling us how he put all his money in offshore accounts, just laying it on thick and thicker. It was amazing; the words just flowed without hesitation. Unbelievable! At one point, he pointed to an area of farmland several hundred acres and said that he had cleared the land and gave it to local poor farmers to help them out. Then he pointed to a man-made catfish pond and proceeded to tell us how he started a new fish industry, and he sells them to the Chinese. I wondered if he believed all this or was he testing us to see just how gullable we were.

Getting back to the planes, General Lee was pushed back in the weeds looking worst for wear with vines growing over it and pieces of old equipment lying all around it. In the middle of all this stuff was one of those old Ag Cats I had seen earlier. Ron proudly showed us how he had mounted this huge diesel engine that had come off a logging skid loader tight up against the firewall. He had a turbine engine mount that encompassed the engine and stuck out another three feet in the front of the engine. A nose cone from Pratt and Whitney 450 with part of a crankshaft was bolted on the front of the mount. To connect the engine to the nose cone was a PTO shaft, much like my tractor has to run the bush hog. To help balance this, he had a big battery hanging right in front of the tailwheel. An array of other things hung all over the plane, such as radiators and oil coolers. Ron told us that he had already enlisted several restaurants to save him cooking oil, and his plan was to fly the plane running on french fry oil. He hadn't been able to get over 1500 rpms out of it, but he had some ideas about getting it to work.

A few years later, while I was helping Dave, Ron came riding up in a homemade trike; it looked pretty cool from a distance. As he got closer, I could see he hadn't changed much. The back wheels of the trike were fairly large and looked to be on an axle from a pickup truck with a 2x12 board holding the back to the front that came off some kind of moped. He was sitting on top of a generator; next to that, there were car batteries. The vehicle was a true hybrid. It ran on electric. When the batteries got low, he would reach down, pull the rope, and the generator would take over. Once again, he made his invention work, but as always, it could use some refinement. The guys said he was living in an old camper down one of the dirt roads and would move from time to time as the county would get on his case. But he has never lost that trademark spirit, and I still envision him at the top of his game dancing to that Carolina beach music wearing, gold chains and that navy blue sport jacket with the Pratt and Whitney insignia.

SINCE the beginning of this adventure, my grandson, Kris, has been my sidekick. The first time I took him for a plane ride, he was about seven, and boy was that a disaster. As soon as the plane lifted off at the point of no return he started screaming and flailing his arms and legs around. It was all I could do to get the plane around the pattern and land. Since then, he has gotten used to flying, even sometimes wanting me to clown around. He would ride in the jump plane sitting on the floor since it didn't have seats asking me, "Can you do that weightless thing again." His first job helping me get started was to take care of our pets while we went to Bainbridge for my flight training.

After I came home, Kris and I would go to farm auctions where we bought gas pumps, water tanks, big gas tanks, hoses, a trailer, etc. Then we spent days building a mix and load station. The load station was a trailer made from half of an old mobile home frame, covered with salt-treated decking. On the front end, we built an 8x8 storage shed with a small side hatch that, when opened, a generator would slide out. We mounted a thousand-gallon gas tank that had been an underground tank in the middle, but looked pretty good painted up. And next to that sat two bulk tanks for water, complete with a float valve. On the back, we mounted an old red fire chief gas pump. Between that and the water tanks were a load pump, a bunch of valves, and the water pump. On the other back edge was a mop sink and inductor with a flush out pipe. Both the sink and inductor had foot pedals to turn on the water, and all this left just enough room in the middle to walk around. We even had premade steps to plop down when we got to the location. All this was done at my friend's storage lot behind his plumbing and heating business, next to the dumpster, and between all his trucks.

Finally one Saturday, we hooked up this monstrosity to tow to Bennett airport. It was almost too much weight for the tires, so I put about sixty psi air in the tires, and they still looked flat. By the grace of God, we made it about thirty miles to the farmhouse that we had yet to move into. Then we filled the already overweight trailer with six hundred gallons of water. Lucky I guess, but we made it around the block to Bennett airport. Once we arrived at Bennett's, we used the water and load pump to shoot in a well. I was able to get about forty-five feet deep before I ran out of the water, which was more than enough for this area, and it worked great.

Often Kris would be my sidekick as I spent the whole day riding the back roads passing out drinks and business cards to any farmer that would give me a little piece of time, hoping to generate some interest in my new business. Who knows how much success we had getting new customers, but we always found good places to eat lunch.

After we moved into the farmhouse, Kris would pack his bags as soon as school let out and spend the summers with us until school started back up in the fall. I turned him into a pretty fair mechanic, as we were always fixing things, mostly the planes. That first year in business, while he was about eight, I had landed in the driveway and had the plane in the back yard so that I could change a bad spark plug. Kris was watching as I tried to turn the plug, but it was stuck. Worst yet it was hard to reach behind the carburetor heat, so mostly talking to myself, I said, "Ah, maybe I better leave this until tomorrow. I have to fly tonight." Not being satisfied I said, "I'll just give it one more try," and sure as hell, "snap," the plug broke off in the hole. With that, I threw a major shit fit, cursing and yelling. I threw all my tools across the yard. Poor Kris went running in the house to Kay, really upset. He had never seen Papa like that before.

As Kris was getting older, at about fourteen I tried to keep him interested in mechanics to help him stay out of trouble. I had pointed out a rusty, 53 Chevy beside the highway on our way home from the Cambridge Airport. "Wouldn't that be great to fix up?" I had sparked his interest and we tried to look at the truck, but there were mean dogs around it, so we left a note in the mailbox. A couple of days later, the guy called and would sell the truck. I asked Kris how he would pay for this; he thought maybe I could loan him the money. Finally, we agreed that he could paint the barn to earn enough for the truck. We met the guy who owned it, and he moved the dogs. Now able to get up close, the thing was a whole lot rustier than I pictured. I told Kris, why don't we hold out for a truck that's in better shape? But now that I had gotten Kris interested, he wouldn't let go. The guy took us up to his house to get the papers. All around the decrepit house, the yard looked like the city dump, but we didn't say anything. Still, the guy said that it may look rough outside, but inside it was "Better Homes and Garden all the way." We just waited outside; I didn't want to go in and risk catching a disease. After we towed the truck home, Kris wanted to see if it would run. The guy had told us that the engine had been rebuilt, but they never got it started some twenty years ago. We hooked up a battery and rigged up a milk jug full of gas to the carburetor. The engine would turn but nothing. I started to check the timing and spark. Instead, I decided to try something else. I reversed the spark plug wires thinking of the many times I have seen guys put engines together with the timing one hundred and eighty degrees off. Zoom, it started right away. It was running a little rough at first until I tuned it, but in those couple minutes of running, it shook a pile of rust out of the doors onto the running boards two inches high. It was going to be a long road to restoring this rust bucket!

Kris was getting pretty good at changing out blown cylinders, which seemed to break way too often. After he begain working on that rust bucket truck, he became pretty good at welding and built two load trucks. He completed the first one at age 14 and the second a year later, so now I had three load trucks and a hood loader if I really needed it. I liked the smaller load trucks because I could tow them with my pickup by myself to the jobs and didn't require insurance or registering. During the seeding season, after I had finished flying for the day, I would hook up a load truck to the pickup, stop at Burger King, and eat dinner while hauling the load truck to the next day's job without having to have someone else bring me home. With more trucks, I would put one at each hot spot until the season was over, which made things easier and enabled us to salvage parts of a day. If we finished early at one location, we could quickly start elsewhere for the last couple of hours of the day without moving equipment.

That next fall while Kris was out of school on Veterans Day, he and a friend got in a real bad accident with a four-wheeler, and he sustained a head injury. He was in a coma for a while, having operations on his head, in the hospital for many months, and the better part of another year going back and forth to A.I. DuPont for rehabilitation. I can still remember him just out of the hospital, still with his head all bandaged up, guiding me and the big front-end loader with my new hangar door to put in place. Together we had the 50 foot wide high fold-door mounted and going up and down in forty-five minutes. The brain injury did change Kris some. He was no longer the jovial fun-loving jokester kid and now would take most things way too seriously. One of the things that changed was sometimes good and other times a pain, but he seemed to have a heightened ability to see details; this ability sometimes was helpful. He would make a good aircraft inspector; he could just glance at something for a second and point out microscopical cracks or missing washers, loose pieces, or any other defects. However, sometimes he would lose sight of the big picture. This extra ability was a big help to me most of the time. Occasionally, it would drive me nuts, like when I would spend a whole day painting something and thought I had done the perfect job. (For some reason I have a hang up about spray painting things, always trying to get that perfect job, and never getting it, kinda like trying to get that perfect golf swing.) Kris would just glance at it and point out all the flaws.

As I was finishing up construction on the new hangar, a guy named Tom came puttering up my driveway in an old Datsun sports car and explained that it cost too much to keep his plane at the county airport, and could he keep his plane here? Thinking sure, I just spent all the time and effort so some strange guy could just come along and use it. I said no way, I wasn't going to push his plane out of my way every time I use mine or push mine out of the way every time he wanted to use his. Thinking that this just gives someone the right to come and go on my property anytime they please, and besides, this guy seems strange. Funny how things work out; many years later, Tom would become my best friend.

Tom was a little extravagant. Somewhere in the '70s after he acquired the things he wanted, such as a plane and fast car, he decided that if you don't want for much, you will not have to work much. After that, he quit his job and never had a full-time job since. He was a good mechanic, and from time to time, he would fix some cars in his backyard for money or favors. Once Tom explained to me that sometimes he would fix cars for the girls in the red-light district for favors, he went on to explain that each party gets what they want, and that he wouldn't have to risk giving away half of his belongings or pay alimony the rest of his life for just an hour or so of fun. Somehow it sounded sensible to me. Tom never used more electricity than the minimum amount the electric company charges for reading the meter, and the power company was always changing the meter thinking that it was broken. Once I gave him a Tim's Aerial Applications hat with a nice Ag Cat and business name embroidered on it. When I stopped by his house, I saw that he had cut the top out and mounted a drop light, so it looked like a coal miner's hat, except it had a cord. He used it to work in the garage so he wouldn't use the electric to light up the whole garage. I said, "For crying out loud, Tom, I would have given you the cheap hats that are printed in ink." Because he didn't have a full-time job, he was the perfect help since I never knew when the jobs would come in. Tom did a beautiful job rebuilding and painting his Piper 140. It took him years, and it was done one wing at a time in his living room.

One day he asked if he could assemble an ultralight and test it at my place. He had gotten it in trade for painting some guy's truck. It took him a month, and I helped him buy the sail envelops in trade for working on my planes. Finally, he was ready to test fly it. All day while I was working in the shop, I could hear the two-stroke engine going up and down the runway, yeing dingdingding, yeing dingdingding, which it sounded like a chain saw. He would get up to speed, lift off about a foot, and cut the power. After a day of listening to this, I was getting annoyed, so I took the golf cart out to the runway and asked, "Tom, are you going to fly that or what?" He answered, "I am getting up my nerve." All I could think was the engine must be good as I've heard it all day, so I made him get out, and jumped in and took off in a huff. Then it dawned on me, I had never flown an ultralight, or worst yet I never checked out the way he put it together, so I just did one big circle around the farm and landed. It turned out Tom did a great job. The next day Tom showed up wearing a parachute. I asked him what's up? He said he was going to fly his new toy. I told Tom, "You'll never be able to get out." He then pulled a knife out and told me he planned to cut the straps that hold the seat and fall out the bottom. I convinced him that it was much safer to ride the thing down than it would be to try using the antique parachute with huge gauges mounted on it that looked as if they belonged in a 1950 pickup truck.

Tom worked on the planes, drove trucks, loaded planes, helped with everything for quite a few years, and was included in our family events. After a few years, we built a place for him to put his plane, and he became a regular for spaghetti dinners. Tom was pretty much happy-go-lucky, except the time he was mixing for me and he wiped his face with a rag covered with warrior (pyrithiamine), which burns like hell and gets worst when washing with water. Recently Tom got sick, and we lost Tom. All of us miss him very much!

It has been a joy to deal with all the farmers I have met over the years; many of them have crossed the line from customer to friend. By in large, most of the farmers are honest, hardworking people. Not long ago I stopped by a farm to look at a field I had to spray. The farmer was more interested if Kay and I were coming to his son's birthday party than if or when I would spray his job.

However, there are always those few. My first week in business I was sitting at a table in a farmer's shop, and the father told me about 73 acres he wanted me to spray, when the son corrected the father stating that it was 78 acres. Then I actually saw the father kick the son under the table and tell the son that he was mistaken, it was 73 acres. I pretended not to see, (they pay by the acre), but it came up to 78 acres when I did the job.

DURING seeding season, I made arrangements to use a farmer's harvested cornfield for a runway to do his cover crop and meet him in the morning. Right after that, I was to meet his cousin right down the road to see his fields. As we pulled out a dirt lane, the cousin pulled up, so we all got out of the pickups and met standing at the dirt driveway. Barry, the cousin that just arrived, turned to me, pointing at Kurt standing next to me and said, "Tell him he is a land thief." Clearly, he was trying to suck me into some kind of family dispute. Luckily, Kurt was a really laid back kinda guy, and Barry couldn't pick a fight. Couple of things I learned: I won't assume families with the same last name all get along together, and not to use a dirt road for a landing strip, where in the middle you must cross a culvert pipe that is only a foot wider than the wheels!

Chapter 14
The "A" Team

Careful what you wish for, or so I'd heard. One year, like most, we were overloaded with work for the cover crop program, so Dave and John showed up to help. Dave with his turbine Thrush and John in a 600 Air Tractor. Dave's plane used too much runway to stop on my shorter satellite runways, and John's used too much runway to take off. Because of this, I gave them the better work in my own backyard, and I had to do the not-so-good work elsewhere. I was getting frustrated that morning because it had taken a lot of time to get them started; it was already 10:30, and I hadn't flown yet and was still forty-five minutes to the strip were my plane sat.

With Kay and Tom in the pickup, I sped down the driveway, turned onto the road, when Kay starts making some kind of grunting noises. Was she constipated or what? So I turn to her and asked, what's wrong? She replied that she had left our sandwiches on the kitchen counter. Feeling the pressure that Dave and John were making money and I wasn't making a penny and doing all the work, I blurted out f--- the sandwiches were going to work. A married man might understand better, but with all the whimpering that came next from Kay, I jammed on the brakes to stop and turn around, but the pedal went to the floor and the truck didn't stop. Now with no brakes, I pulled to the side of the road; frustrated, I slammed the truck in reverse, gunned it, and turned around and went home, totally forgetting about the trailer I was pulling. With a big crunch sound, I jackknifed the truck and trailer, caving in the whole backside of the truck. I wish I could say that was the end of this story, but when we did get back home, Kay didn't want to let me haul the trailer with her smaller pickup truck. Finally, she and Tom saw that I was about one second away from going absolutely postal, so she gave in, and eventually we got to work, where I received the silent treatment for the rest of the day.

MOST people have heard all the in-law jokes, like the definition of a "mixed emotion" is like the guy that puts on a great big smile when he finds out his mother-in-law drove off a cliff, but then the smile quickly turns to a frown when he learns she was driving his brand-new Mercedes. Well, in my case, that couldn't be farther from the truth, my in-laws are just great! My father-in-law, Cade, and my wife are the ground crew when we cover crop seed, starting mid-August through late October, from sunup to sundown every day.

One day working out of a neighboring airport and set up on the end of the T-hangers, flying a 450 Ag Cat seeding, and Jeff a friendly competitor set up just a few hundred feet away at the end of the next set of T-hangers with his turbine Thrush, we both had a tractor trailer load to do. The work can get monotonous sometimes, and just to break up the monotony, my

Jeff struck up a conversation on the radio and asked, "Tim, how many acres do you do each flight?" I answered about twelve or thirteen. He said "Oh my that's terrible! Gees that's terrible! Oh my god that's terrible!" He must have said the word terrible a dozen times, then he stated, "I do about thirty-three acres each time." I knew he was on the beginning end of the large payments for that shiny brand-new airplane, so when he got done with his terribleness, I answered, "Do you want to know what's not terrible?" Then he replied, "Don't even say it, I know what you are going to say." I called him back and said, "I can't help it, but what's not terrible is that this old bird I am flying is bought and paid for. Whatever I make today goes in my blue jeans." Across the way, they had three younger fellows loading that Turbine. I had the "A" team going strong for me, my eighty-some-year-old father-in-law and my sixty-some-year-old wife loading me; all day long, we did at least two loads to their one and finished our truck first.

After running a construction company with many employees and headaches, and later running the pharmaceutical plant with a hundred or so employees and more headaches, I wanted to enjoy whatever was next. My business was modeled after Floyd's barbershop on the Andy Griffin show. My competitor has gone on to have many turbine aircraft and does a great business. Whose to say which plan is best? I suppose we have both been successful in our own ways.

Good old Bob, he had agreed to fly my 600 and help me on a seeding job in Somerset County. I had borrowed John Anderson's runway in the heart of the job; in fact, some of the seeding was on his land on each side of the runway. The runway was narrow, with a gravel lane cutting through the middle, and we set up our load area next to the lane. It was really the only area large enough for the trucks. Somehow, I manage to finagle Cade into hooking the battery cables that ran the gas pump to his new SUV. This was no easy task, for Cade was one who kept everything perfect. His home was the neatest and cleanest on the block, there wasn't one leaf left lying in his yard, and he wiped off his car after he parked in the garage every time. I had pulled my plane off to the side while waiting for Bob to finish gassing up and go on. When he started to taxi out, swinging around on that gravel lane, he really put the power to it. Just sitting there helpless in my plane, watching the great big cloud of dust and gravel that left the tail of the plane spread all over Cade's shiny new car. Worst yet, Cade had left his door open. I could see this cloud swirling around inside of the car, all over the nice leather seats.

Later, when it was time for me to gas up, Kay and her father wouldn't give me gas, and Cade's SUV was parked far away. I met some resistance when asked why don't you hook up my pickup instead. Hindsight being what it is, I think I lost the battle when I slipped up and dropped the F-bomb. Bob came over and got in the middle and calmed all three of us down, and we went back to work. Since the job was to take three or four days, we left the planes there and drove back and forth. Bob drove separately since he lived in a different direction, and Kay, Cade, and me in Cade's not-so-clean car. Obviously, Kay and Cade were still mad at me, so just like the old TV commercial, it was so quiet you could hear a pin drop. I received the silent treatment for a couple more days and don't even think Kay was going to fix me dinner. I still can't figure out how things got twisted around for the life of me; Bob came out of it like Prince

Charming and I ended up the bad guy. I was not the one who filled the car full of dust.

I first met Cade when I was dating Kay. She took me to their home, where he was down in a big hole digging a swimming pool. I introduced myself and jumped in and volunteered to help. Wanting to impress him, I was sure to throw out a shovel scoop for every one of his scoops. After a while, I started to get winded, but he just kept on shoveling. It was starting to get unbearable as I ran out of steam, I was twenty-one, and he was in his mid-fifties. I silently vowed not to quit until he quit. Just about the time I almost passed out, he paused and said, let's take a break.

Kay had moved into a two-story house across from an old Victorian house that I bought just a couple months after getting out of high school and was attempting to fix up. It was a nice warm summer day when I glanced across the street to see this beautiful brunette in short white shorts and man did she look good! So, I beelined over and offered to help, but got a snotty response. "No, my father is helping me." I walked back to my side of the street, thinking, "You stuck up b----!" and for the longest time, I wouldn't look that way or acknowledge her.

I'm not going into the stories of how she called the cops on all the loud parties that emulated from my side of the street as I enjoyed my single life, since she still denies this, but somehow, we got together. While we were dating, I would spend a lot of time at her house, if not all of my time, since my house was under repair with no interior, heat, or anything. One day I strung a phone line from her attic across the road to my attic and down to her laundry room. Her mom, who wanted to be sure everything was proper, would call Kay, and after speaking to her for a while, she would ask Kay, "Where's Tim? I want to talk to him." Kay would tell her that Tim must be over at his house. Kay's mom would hang up, and just seconds later, my phone would ring just a few feet away, hidden in the laundry room. I would answer, I'd talk a couple minutes, and Kay's mom, now satisfied that I was where I belonged, would hang up happy. When Kay's parents came to visit, Cade who worked for the phone company was standing on the front porch, he looked up at the wire strung between our homes and just winked at me.

I was building a spec house to sell in my hometown of Seaford. I had just met the fellows from the power company, and they showed me where I had to trench in the lines to hook to their transformer. Digging away with the backhoe, Mr. Miller showed up from the phone company. He asked me if I had called Miss Utility, I told him that I hadn't, but the guys from the power company showed me where everything is. Mr. Miller told me that I had to stop and get Miss Utility to mark everything. I said, you're here now, can't you just tell me where things are. He can come across as pretty abrasive for those who don't know Mr. Miller, so between that and the backhoe's diesel engine running that we were already hollering over, we went back and forth until something got into me. I got on my high horse and blurted out, "It's my land, and I'll dig it if I want to!" Mr. Miller just stormed away, and I went back to work. I didn't even take two scoops before I pulled up a wire. I hoped it was anything but a phone wire, but no such luck. Worst than that, it was a big one. I had knocked out phone service to all of Woodside Manor's hundred homes and more. It was already going on four o'clock, so I decided I would go ask Cade for help as soon as he got off work, since he did these kind of repairs for the phone company. I found Cade, told him that I had a small problem and needed his help. He just turned to me and said, "It's your land, and you'll dig it if you want to." Then he went on to explain this is too big of a problem and would have to go through the phone company. For the next couple of days, Cade worked out there with a big phone truck and he had one of those yellow tent thing set up over the hole, like I see along the road in work areas. He kept telling me that I was going to get one hell of a bill. For many years Cade would give me pens, rulers, and pads of paper, all with Miss Utility and the 800 number printed on it, for Christmas or birthdays, and maintained that I was going to get a hell of a bill. I never got the bill; he probably fixed the paperwork but wasn't about to tell me.

Cade was a joy to work with. He never got angry with me, even though I probably pulled his chain a few times. The worst he would do is throw in a extra "Okay," so when I would get an answer, Okay Tim, I knew I'd crossed the line. Sadly, Cade passed away a couple years ago. I could have never wished for any better of a father-in-law!

Chapter 15
What A Difference A Day Makes

That last week of the year can get crazy. Due to bad weather, the state had extended the cover crop deadline and we were now in overtime. I had brought in two other planes to help and put them at a busy satellite strip. What a disaster. Normally I would leave Kay there to take charge while I worked elsewhere. Since this was beyond the original completion date, Kay had made a hair appointment, and she was done for the season and wouldn't back down, there was no changing her mind. So, I left the pilots maps and instructions, like (do the blue truck first, then do the green truck, and the big red one goes with this job last).

I dropped in on them midday to find they had mixed up the wheat and barley trucks with the two brother farmers who hate each other. Worse than that, when I got there, Burt, the certified seed grower from that area, showed up and was raising hell with me. He was so upset he damn near walked into a spinning prop. My pilot had been turning around over a field that he had planned on planting certified barley. Apparently, Burt stood at the edge of the field waving his arms to make him go away, but the pilot thought he was the farmer they were working for being friendly. As the pilot finished, he buzzed Burt and waved, which totally infuriated Burt. I committed a cardinal offense by telling Burt that we were done in that area, but that if anything was wrong, I would make it right, but I had to keep going as this is our last day of the deadline, and said I'd get up with him later. What I did wrong as any successful businessman knows, and I knew better, is that I should have shut down my engine and given him the time and attention needed. I have dealt with him in the past and he had a reputation for being hard to deal with. The farmer I was seeding for had offered to spray Burt's field just in case, since nothing had been planted yet, but he wouldn't accept it. Monthly we walked the field, and not a single plant was out of the furrows. The way the wind was blowing when the cover crop was being applied, blew the seeds away from Burt's field, in fact, the first hundred feet of the field we were working on was bare. Ordinarily I would have been mad at the pilot, but in this case I was glad. We were sure that not a seed had landed on his field and felt that all was good.

But that next spring, I got a letter from a lawyer threatening to sue. So, I went to see the seed grower and his son who did the farming. They had a report written by the son's father-in-law, who was a state seed inspector, stating that the field had been contaminated, especially along the runway. I am guessing that he misunderstood his son-in-law instructions involving a plane, since there are no runways were near the field. Knowing that nobody wins if it goes to court, and not wanting to send bad vibes to the rest of the farmers that I don't stand behind my work, and since I felt that I didn't handle this right in the beginning, I opted to reach a settlement. They wanted me to pay the price between the normal grain price and the certified seed price. They figured that it would come to nineteen thousand something, but I said since they didn't have to process it or package it the price should be less. We went back and forth, finally something clicked inside of me. "If you are going to screw me, go all the way," and I rounded the check up to twenty thousand and said, "You must need it pretty bad if you're willing to tell these stories." After I paid them, they tried to defuse the tension by telling some hard-luck stories. The son didn't know when to shut up by telling me they lost another field from flooding and used the field in question as normal grain, in order to meet what they had under contract.

Feeling cheated, and really screwed, I couldn't get this off my mind over the next couple of days. I had printed out Google Earth pictures with dates to show that they lied about when they planted, and much other info. I really was getting consumed by this injustice. For days I was thinking about this, and I was flying like a madman, slamming the stick around, almost running into things. Finally, I caught myself: (if you don't get over this, you are probably going to wreck), so I said a prayer, "Please lord, let me just forget this. I no longer want justice or to get even, just put it behind me and let me forget it."

When I landed, my phone went off: it was Jimmy Harding, a farmer and logger. I spray watermelons for both Jimmy and his brother Howard. Like most watermelon growers, they love to plant in tight places, like between buildings and trees, as this keeps the wind from twisting off the vines in the early stages of growth. This year Jimmy had his fields in the worst places. I didn't know how they even turn the tractor around in these small fields, much less how I was getting the plane in there without killing myself, but I did. However, he also had one field about ½ mile long and narrow with tall trees lining the long sides and the ends relatively open, and that made for easy spraying. Jimmy wanted to know if I could start spraying that long field crossways, which would mean fighting tall pine trees and taking a really long time to do. I thought about it for a little bit, and then I answered, "Jimmy, when I see those logging trucks of yours going down Route 50 with the logs loaded sideways, I'll start spraying that field sideways." With that, I could hear Jimmy and Howard laughing and carrying on, as they like to sit in the packing house in the afternoon and have a beer or two. This made me stop to think that there are still many people who I enjoy working with. Still, I do think the Lord has a real sense of humor to make Jimmy Harding the answer to my prayer. I'll have to admit it worked; I forgot about being cheated by the seed grower. Truly the Lord works in strange ways!

ONE Friday morning towards the end of May, I climbed out of bed early, and rooted through the clothes hanging in the closet, looking for a good shirt that didn't have ink spots around the pocket, and matching dress pants, as I did every morning going to work at Trinity Laboratories and Trigen Labs (the pill-plant). Got in my small beat-up economy car, stopped at Dunkin' Donuts and got my coffee, just as I had done for the last ten years, then drove to Salisbury, unlocked the doors, turned off the alarm, and did my walk-around, taking notes. Then sat down at my desk to write a short list for each department supervisor, trying to sip my coffee in peace. Most mornings I would get there a good hour ahead of time because I enjoyed the peace and quiet with time to get my thoughts together. This alone time was important to me. But this morning would be no different from any other, a couple of ladies who worked in the cleanroom were waiting for me to unlock the door. I should be happy to have such great conscientious people who take pride in their work, but I really just wanted to be left alone, just for a little bit, but just like most days, the ladies wanted to talk to me, and I wouldn't be able to finish the cold coffee until the ten o'clock break. The earlier I came to work, the earlier they would show up; there was no winning! I overheard the one lady tell the other to watch out, Tim's in a bad mood today. The other lady asked, how do you know he's in a bad mood? "I could see the lines on his forehead this morning when he opened the door," the first lady answered. In my defense, that's not true, I started every day in a good mood, and some days it lasted all day, and other days someone would pull my chain early. I do want to say of all the things I was involved in with the plant, from constructing the building, setting up the equipment, filling the place with people, setting up systems, adding on to the plant, getting things running, etc. the only real thing that I am proud of was finding some of the great people that worked there. At the time I was writing this, some employees now turned friends had been there twenty-five years, so I guess it's a good thing I never got to drink my coffee in peace!

Before taking on Trinity, I had mostly worked construction, with much of it outdoors. I always loved the freedom of working in the open spaces, meeting new people daily, and the traveling that goes with it. I have always considered that a great benefit. But now my job kept me locked in a building. There were some days I would go to work in the dark and go home in the dark, never seeing the light of day. In the winter, I would go out to my car after work, and it may have snow on it, and I never saw the snow fall. But this day was different. At lunchtime, I was given a cake, and everybody was wishing me well. My secretary had gotten a toy plane and put it on the cake. She had broken the prop off and stuck it in the cake next to the plane, just to remind me of the two weeks I missed work getting my first plane home. At the end of the day, I said all my goodbyes, then cleaned out my desk, took my pictures off the wall, turned on the alarm, locked the doors, and drove home.

As I waited to pull into the apartment driveway of our not-so-great neighborhood, I waited like every other night for the crowd of characters that seemed to hang out on the street at all hours to let me pass. Someone called out to me, as they had many times before, "Hey you white mother f-----, what's you's doing here?" I hurried into the second floor dump of an apartment that we had moved into for the winter. The plaster was falling off the walls and ceiling, the bathroom was down the unheated hallway, and the heat that wouldn't regulate would get either hotter than hell or cold as ice every ten minutes. The bedroom window was in the front near the street, so all night long, all you could hear was, "boom key-thump boom, boom key-thump boom" of the boom boxes. Some of the cars stereo's base was so loud that you could feel the vibrations in bed, and this would go on most of the night.

In the weeks leading up to this particular day whatever time I could find, I would ride the back roads, and pass out business cards to every farmer I could find. There's a bit of an art to doing sales work with farmers. First of all, do not drive up in a car, especially a shiny one. It is best to drive up in an older pickup, but not too old, and it is even better if you can drive it through some mud puddles first. I would fill up a big cooler with ice and drinks. The best results were if it appeared to be an impromptu meeting, like catching them in the field. Catching a farmer turning around on an end row could be tricky because they don't like to stop, as they may have been fighting adjustments on the planter or whatever and finally got it right, and now some butt hole wants them to stop! I found that giving them a cold drink and apologizing for stopping them worked well. As I always say, the drink is for stopping them and not to get their business, and they normally would forgive me. Somewhere between the third and fourth time you stop by with a cold drink, they will start to talk business. At the first meeting I would give out a business card and tell them that I would love a chance to prove myself. After that, I wouldn't talk business anymore unless they did. I would cry poor (which is true), but they can't really think you're poor. It is hard to explain if they really thought you were poor, they wouldn't deal with you, so they have to believe you're doing okay but just crying poor. I find most farmers do this fairly well. After the poor routine, then you talk about women. You never push yourself. I used to tell them that it is tough to sell myself because my competitors all do good work, and wish it wasn't so; in that way, I'd have a chance to tell you I am better. Lastly, I learned that they don't like to deal with people from the big city. Seaford, my hometown with the DuPont factory, and Salisbury where I just moved to were considered "big cities." Hebron is a small town closer to Bennett Airport than Salisbury, so I had it printed on my business card, even though my address was Salisbury. When I said I was from Hebron, they seemed to accept me better. Freestyle, (a term used by American Pickers on

TV,) where they would randomly ride the back roads, and stop to talk to anyone that might sell antiques. This seemed to be one of the best chances of getting a farmer that may use my service, I would stop to talk to anyone on a tractor, especially the ones with double tires. One day while passing out cards, just around the corner from the airport, I drove down a long farm lane, and an older lady met me in the driveway. After explaining my mission, she told me that the farmland was rented out and she was just there having an open house to rent the farmhouse. So, we rented the house, and years later we would buy the farm.

Getting back to my story, after having my cake that Friday (last day at the pill-plant), we moved into the farmhouse that next day. Monday morning, I got up and walked to the closet, only this time I picked out comfortable blue jeans and a favorite tee shirt, went downstairs, and Kay handed me a cup of coffee. Outside it was sunny but just cool enough to put on a light jacket. There wasn't a soul insight, just a few birds chirping in the trees dotted around the farmhouse, and then big empty fields in all directions. I climbed in my 1930 Ford Model A that I love to drive and chugged my way over to Bennett's airport, where I started up my biplane with the WWII round engine. There is something romantic about seeing that little puff of gray smoke as the round engine slowly starts to chug, and chug, chug, and chug-ah, chug-ah, chug-ah, chug-ah, as it comes to life. I sprayed all morning. Most of the work was in sight of the Chesapeake Bay, where even a postcard couldn't capture the magnificence of the scenery. Later I took a picture showing all the fields, trees, beaches, rivers, and the Bay, this just unbelievable view, so I could send it to the folks back at the pill-plant office, writing on it, "This is the view out of my new office window."

What A Difference A Day Makes

Around ten o'clock, it started to get a little breezy, so I stopped spraying, got in the Model A, and chugged my way to Berlin to tow banners up and down the beach over Ocean City. Now working for Bob, I was flying a 180 horsepower Piper Super Cub with no windows or door. It's like riding in an open Jeep, just a real fun plane to fly. Unfortunately, we hardly ever get to fly the Super Cubs empty when they perform great. Almost all of the time, we are dragging banners, and the plane is a real dog. Behind Bob's parents' home is the runway and field where during the summer teams of high school kids roll out and set up the banners, but today only one person was doing the ground-work. This area of activity is referred to as the farm. The beach is about four miles away. As soon as I pop up with the banner, I can see all the tall buildings silhouetted by the ocean, a beautiful view. The run starts at the inlet at the south end of the city. As you approach, to the left, you see the city on a narrow strip of land sandwiched between Assawoman Bay, which is lined with boat docks, and the gold sand touching the Atlantic Ocean on the opposite side. On the right is the harbor with several canals, the first full of the larger fishing boats that have tall out riggers, lot of antennas, and a big roll of fishing net. The next couple canals are full of smaller charter boats with tall fishing poles, and the shacks that service the fleet of boats. The harbor gives way to Assateague Bay, which separates the mainland from the narrow untouched beach that goes as far as you can see. That Assateague beach goes past Chincoteague, Virginia, and the wild ponies live all along that beach and park. Some days the ponies will make their way towards that north end and we can see them. Straight ahead, in the inlet neatly spaced out, there are a half dozen char-ter boats in line heading out to sea. As I make my way over the ocean, turning left to run along the beach, looking further up the ocean, the condominiums and hotels are lined up along the bright gold colored sandy beach going north as far as I can see. I passed colorful parachutes, almost as high as my plane, attached to a long rope, with a boat down below pulling them. As I make my way up the beach full of thousands of people and different colored umbrellas, sometimes you can see schools of fish, or groups of dolphins that just effortlessly rise out of the water and back down again, like they are playing a game of follow the leader, and sometimes I even see manatees that barely look like they are moving. At the end of Ocean City is Fenwick Island Delaware that is building up too, but not as much as Ocean City. The end of the route is marked by the white historic Fenwick Island Lighthouse. As I go to push the power to full, the knob doesn't move far because the plane is already almost full power, at forty-five mph. Once the plane reached eight hundred feet, I made a left turn over the beach and headed for the farm. I crossed over Assawoman Bay, then passed the Isle of Wright. I looked back again at Ocean City across the bay and took more pictures. I followed a river just north of Ocean Pines and passed over a little island full of pine trees called Piney Island that we use for a checkpoint. I called the ground crew and told them that I was passing Piney Island since it is only two minutes away. Back at the farm, I dropped the banner, threw out another rope with a hook, swung around, and picked up another banner and headed back to the beach.

After a day of dragging rags, I got back in the Model A, drove back to Bennett Airport, flew more crop dusting jobs until dark, and then chugged my way home. At that time, I was just consumed with my desire to fly, so it was a fantastic day. I pulled in the half-mile-long driveway, not passing a soul along the way. When I got out of the car it was very quiet. All I could hear was the crickets chirping and I smelled a charcoal grill. Kay told me to sit in a lawn chair under the big tree. As I sat there, Kay gave me a frosted glass mug filled with Heineken beer and then brought me a charcoal-cooked steak dinner. I think, I even had sex that night. What a difference a day can make! In just one day's time, I had gone from a house and neighborhood I hated, coupled with a dull, boring routine, and a job that I had grown tired of, to have the Best Day of My Life!

I tell this story occasionally to different people when I sense they are down and out, or at the end of their rope. There is no telling how good tomorrow can be!

The Learning Curve

The Construction Days (left)

The Pill Plant (below)

The Farmhouse

Kay

Kris's First Plane Ride

Photos

Goodbye, Packard.
Hello, Ag School.

That
Hateful
Red
Pawnee

The Pig

The Ag Cat I
Never Got to Fly

The Learning Curve

My
New
Old
Plane

Doing repairs
in the
Trinity Labs
warehouse
on the
weekends

A little
patchwork
after that
broken tail
wheel

Photos

We're in business now!

Kay mixing

Kris working on the water tanks

The Learning Curve

My nephews checking out the plane.

Grandson Kris Gassing up Age 8

Rebuilding the plane in the barn after first year in business.

Photos

I am gassing up
while Kay is
loading seeds.

She gets a new
hair-do for free.

Tight fit!

I hate it
when it
comes
in bags.

My first 600
working off
a cornfield

Loading
with a hood
loader

Swapping
out an
engine in
a field

Kay loading
that first 600
now with a
new paint
job.

Not only is
the Ag Cat
all redone
but I have
a new load
truck.

Photos

This gives new meaning to do it yourself.

Cade driving

Me working

Kay is always in the middle of whatever is going on.

The Learning Curve

The Runaway
Irrigation

Never did
get to go
fishing.

Photos

That
Broken
Landing
Wire

Jerry Abbott
(center)
fixing a
blown
cylinder
while I (left)
watch.
Bob (right) is
supervising.

The Learning Curve

Hate it when
the truck
doesn't dump.

Nothing to say but
oh shit!

Wonder how much
it will cost this
time?

Oops!

Photos

Road trip:
Kris and I got a
whole Ag Cat on a
trailer and hauled
it halfway across
the USA.

Kris painting
the barn to earn
money to buy
a pickup truck.

All done.

His reward -
a 1953 rust bucket

The Learning Curve

Cub Scouts
came for a visit.

Our friend Tom

Photos

Kris giving Cade a ride.

Flying off a bean field - Cade getting a little prop blast

Cade the pool shark in the room built upstairs in the hangar

Kay taking some time off

The Learning Curve

My second 600 Ag Cat loaded with the truck Kris built at age 14.

Kay didn't believe me when I said it could fly again.

Once was a beautiful Ag Cat

Photos

Good friend, Dave
Barrett, working on
Bill Bennett's T-6

Perfect Day

Hanging out with
the grandkids

Bonus Pictures
What I did in the off season

Photos

CPSIA information can be obtained
at www.ICGtesting.com
Printed in the USA
BVHW050339100623
665697BV00001B/2

9 781628 063752